From Far North Norway

Written by Eunice Kanne

Edited by Maurice Crownhart

New Past Press Inc.

From Far North Norway

Illustrated by Diane Wicklund, Grantsburg

Edited by Maurice Crownhart, Grantsburg

Publishing Services:
Editing, Design, Pre-Press Production

New Past Press Inc., Friendship Wisconsin

Carol Ann Podoll, Publishing Assistant

Manufactured in the United States of America

ISBN 0-938627-44-19

Library of Congress Cataloging

F589.G68K355   98-31504
977.5'14--dc21   CIP

Cover illustration by Diane Wicklund features a girl wearing the traditional *bunad* outfit of North Norway.

ACKNOWLEDGEMENTS

I want to thank the many people who have made publication of my writings possible.

First and foremost, were it not for the encouragement and computer skills of Maurice Crownhart, my stories about North Norway would never have become a book.

Then there are the relatives and others in Norway who have helped so willingly. Special thanks to Reidar Thomassen for the many fine stories he collected years ago for our family. They will now live on in this book. A thank you to Kristianne Brandmo for hours spent editing the writings for accuracy and for supplying other factual material. To Gudrun Thomassen, I am grateful for her stories and her answers to my many questions. My appreciation is extended to personnel in the Bardo and Hadsel tourist offices for your help.

Many individuals too numerous to mention have supplied information concerning their families.

I obtained excellent help from our Grantsburg library, which has a wealth of material for family research. Henry Peterson's genealogy collection is remarkable and he has so willingly shared the information. Special thanks to Gordon Larson, whose knowledge of the library's records helped me obtain hard to find Hadsel material.

I particularly want to thank Diane Wicklund for consenting to illustrate the book.

CONTENTS

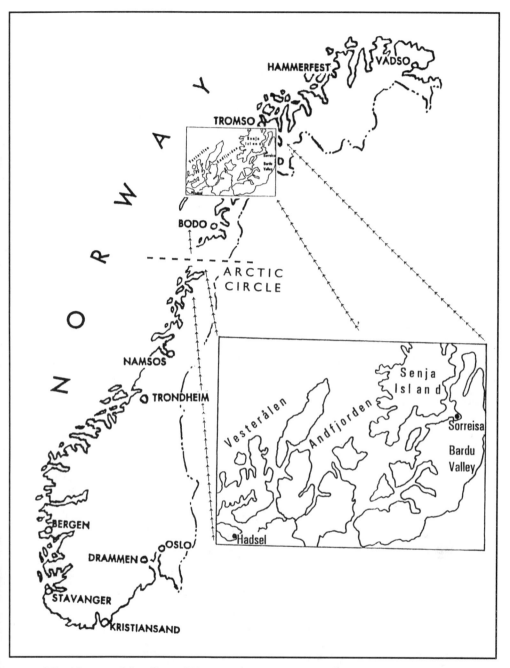

The far north region of Norway was the home of many Grantsburg-area settlers.

PREFACE

Many folks of North Norway ancestry are not aware that their ancestors came from one of the world's most unique places. The three areas I am writing about in this book, places few tourists are taken to, lie well above the Arctic Circle. Beauty is everywhere. It is overwhelming. One is never out of sight of mountains, with their cascading waterfalls, and fjords that sometimes reach far into the land. This is a paradise all its own; one of the world's most beautiful spots.

It is unique in other ways. Lying as it does within the Arctic Circle, they experience the Midnight Sun in summer. In dark winter months they have the best views of Northern Lights. Warmed as they are by the Gulf Stream, it is the only place on earth this far north where crops such as potatoes and some grains are grown. Their average temperatures are not too different from ours.

Today there are countless descendents of early immigrants who came from this Nordland, many in the Grantsburg area. I've put the book together in hopes that these people may learn how their ancestors lived in this beautiful land. The book describes early life in Norway above the Arctic Circle.

Years ago a cousin, Reidar Thomassen, who lives near Sorreisa in the Coastal Area, collected people's stories of early eighteenth century life, from those living on the coast. These I have included. They are too good to be limited to my family history. His stories and those of others are printed in Italics.

Along with my stories and others are included available genealogies of the first two generations of many of these first families who came to Grantsburg in the 1860s. Readers who have family genealogies that are not in Henry Peterson's collection are asked to get theirs to him. They are in the Grantsburg library, where I have received a great deal of help.

As added items of interest, maps of farms settled by early arrivals are included, giving names of those receiving original deeds. There is also a list of a few other early area farmers and where they farmed.

Because of the lack of records, as well as their accuracy, I am sure there are discrepancies and things some think should have been included, but I hope readers will overlook such things.

INTRODUCTION TO NORTH NORWAY

Norway is a long and narrow country stretching from north to south for 13 degrees of latitude. It extends from the 58th parallel at Lindesnes, the most southerly point, up to the 71st parallel at the North Cape. It measures near a thousand miles from south to north, but following the sea-washed coastline in and out of all the fjords and inlets, it would measure 12,500 miles, half way around the equator.

Norway is also one of our most mountainous countries, with some say less than three per cent of its area suitable for cultivating, very little of which is in this North Country. Many of the tallest mountains seem to rise right out of ocean waters bordering western Norway. Mountain peaks, rising farther from shore, form islands found all along the coast. So numerous are these islands that one figure given was 19,000, but others, counting all the smaller ones, say there are thousands more. Totally in the North Country, they form a wall protecting coastal land from open seas, as well as the Arctic. Surrounded as they are by warm Gulf Stream waters, a green belt of plants grows on island mountainsides up to the Arctic Tundra, well above the city of Tromso.

The islands of Senja and Hinnoya boast great gardens, which have lush strawberries in August. The Midnight Sun, with long summer days and, of course, a friendly Gulf Stream, makes this possible. However, even in coastal areas, where the Gulf Stream's effect is felt, there can be snow on the ground in May and as early as September. Weather can change, and snow melts quickly.

This coast is where early Vikings lived. Here they found plenty of fish for food, and thick forests from which wood was cut to build their famous boats and ships. So seaworthy were these ships that Vikings were able to sail far beyond their shores to carry on aggressive raids and captures, and bring about contact with the outside world.

Today these forests are one of Norway's greatest assets. Figures given say that 22 of every 100 acres are in forests. With their shorter summers, it takes about 30 years for a tree to grow to marketable size. The government fosters replacement of trees, so that it will be an ongoing resource.

This beautiful area in North Norway has been known to man for thousands of years. Besides the Vikings, another culture occupied North Norway. Traces of their dwelling sites, rock carving, and arrowheads prove their existence as hunters and fishermen. Today North Norway is occupied by two cultures living peacefully side by side: the Sami, or Laplanders, many with their own language, and the Norwegians, who speak theirs.

THE SAMI

The Sami, or as we termed them in my grade school days, Laplanders, have been around for an unknown length of time. Archeologists have found traces of their culture as far south in Europe as Poland. As other people moved in from the south and east, the Sami withdrew to the north. That they did not absorb the culture and ways of the invaders is evident in their language. It does not contain words for such as "war" or "farming." They have, however, countless words describing nature. They divide the year into eight seasons, and are said to have ninety words describing variations in snow conditions. Reindeer herding is the real mark of their culture.

Today most Sami are living above the Arctic Circle in Norway, Sweden, Finland and Russia. Of an estimated 70,000 Sami, Northern Sweden is thought to have about 17,000, Finland 5,700 and Northern Russia may have 2,000. Norway has an estimated 40,000 to 50,000. (Due to some living a nomadic way of life, they are difficult to count). Most of these in Norway are living in Finnmark fylke (county) which lies to the north of Bardu Valley and Tromso.

These Sami are an ethnic minority in Norway, but also Norwegian citizens, and are native inhabitants much as the Indians are in our country. Today Norway is making great efforts to encourage the Sami to preserve and develop the Sami language, culture and way of life. Sami language is taught in their schools, and museums and cultural centers are now established with Norwegian government support. The world is learning about Sami music (Yoik), about Sami legends, turf huts, folk medicine, reindeer sleds, carved wares and their knowledge of ecology. Best known perhaps is their colorful national dress.

Missionaries began work even before the 1700's and churches were built. It was through encouragement of early church workers that the Sami language was accepted and many works were translated into Sami, including the New Testament, at an early date.

Today there is the Sami Parliament or Assembly, a national body, which is their political representative group. This is their public administration voice in matters important to the Sami people.

They have a great number and variety of legends. One collection written in Sami by J. K. Qvigstad is "Sami Fairytales and Leaboutgends." Now there are novels and many modern authors who are writing in Sami. There are paintings and other examples of pictorial art. Sami language newspapers and magazines are published. Norwegian broadcasts feature programs in Sami from time to time.

The Sami are a short people, four and a half to five and a half feet tall. Early sources of information about the Sami describe them as hunters and skiers who hunted and kept reindeer. Furs were prized while animal hides later became an important commodity. Countries in control of areas they occupied collected taxes from them. In cases where more than one ruling group claimed an occupied area, the Sami might pay taxes twice or more. Dissention was just not a part of their culture.

Early Sami were nomads moving where their reindeer herds found food. This might mean their animals swimming across fjords in May to summer pastures on islands, and back in September or October. In winter they were pastured on higher mountain plateaus, where reindeer searched for moss and lichens on which to feed, often pawing under snow to find it. Reindeer supplied meat and milk, and were their beasts of burden, trained to draw heavy loads over snowy trails. Their milk is very thick and rich (so thick water is added before drinking). It is drawn from animals with some difficulty and in very small quantities, cups not quarts. It is an important food similar to goat's milk, more nutritious than cow's milk.

This way of living has been going on for thousands of years. However, time has brought changes. Reindeer herding is still carried on but has been modernized. Now the chief aim is producing as much meat as possible. Meat from reindeer makes up about one percent of the total meat produced in Norway (1985 figures). It is estimated only ten percent are herding reindeer today.

Instead, Sami are active in many fields of endeavor. Agriculture, trades, many service industries, as well as most professions are their sources of income. Handicrafts are important where there are tourists looking for souvenirs.

Many stories are told of the "magic" power of some Sami people. Few today believe these stories. One of Reidar's stories tells of this friendship between a farm woman living on the coast and a Sami woman. The story follows:

After Kristianna Clementson (Adolph's sister) married Thomas Edvart Thomassen and moved to Sildvik, she had such bad luck with her livestock that both lambs and calves died. Now and then a mature animal perished without anyone being able to find a cause of the deaths.

At that time, before the turn of the century, some Laplanders (Sami) herded their reindeer in summer pastures up in the mountains, which land was part of the Sildvik property. Once in a while one of these Laplanders came down to Sildvik to get a boat ride over the fjord to go to Klauva to shop or trade. Ravna, a Lapp woman, became a good friend of Kristianna.

One day when the weather was fine, Ravna came down and wanted to cross the fjord. Kristianna decided to take the day off, leave the children with a neighbor and row across the fjord with Ravna. It was late in the evening when they returned from Klauva and Kristianna persuaded Ravna to spend the night in Sildvik. In the morning Kristianna took coffee and cakes arranged on a tray to her friend in the upstairs room. When Ravna saw the tray she clapped her hands and exclaimed in broken Norwegian, "Did you ever see the like? As fine as for a queen and even with a saucer." And there, sitting on the edge of the bed, Kristianna talked about her misfortune with her livestock. (A "fosen" in the barn). Ravna said nothing but listened. When she was ready to leave she asked,

"May I see the barns?" Kristianna took her down to the "fjoset." Ravna stood a moment in the middle of the barn floor, then clasped her hands and said, "Avoi, avoi, for the 'envy' you have experienced in your barn, Kristianna." Then she bade my grandmother to leave the barn and go to the house alone. A little later Ravna returned to the house, thanked her hostess and began to climb up the mountain. From that time Kristianna never lost a single animal.

A DIFFERENT PART OF THE WORLD

In Norway, early people found their way farther north as time went on, always making their homes close to the shores, on islands or mainland. Here they were close to the world's richest fishing grounds. Gradually these early settlers in mid-Norway worked their way inland, where they found huge forests. There they could hunt for animals for food and fur for clothing. They found material with which to build their homes. In time these early settlers took to farming the small patches of fertile soil, growing grass to feed a limited number of livestock over the long winter, as well as potatoes and grain for flour. What a welcome addition to the diet the potatoes must have been when they were brought over to Europe from North and South America in the 1700's.

If you choose to visit this area of Norway above the Arctic Circle, you are due for many surprises. The beauty of this area can be overwhelming. Here along the western shores, high mountains plunge abruptly into the sea. Between them their valleys form fjords, which are an extension of the sea. Webster says, "a fjord is a narrow inlet or arm of the sea bordered by steep cliffs, especially in Norway." These often reach far inland, helping to add miles of coastline as well as to make more of Norway accessible to the sea.

In many ways this part of Norway is unique. No other place in the world is like it. First is its great beauty, with mountains, fjords, and waterfalls wherever you look. The few farms, with colorful red barns and white houses, add to the scenery. With the whole of Norway's small population of about four million Norwegians in all the country, much of the area's scenery is untouched, and is in its original condition. One other thing which makes this area unusual is that it is the world's best area in which to view aurora borealis, the Northern Lights. Here they are much more spectacular and higher in the sky than seen in Wisconsin, mainly because the area is so close to the Magnetic Pole. I have read that at their peak, the flashing lights are so powerful that one can read by them, a rare occurrence. Moonlight helps.

We are told Northern Lights are the result of solar particles colliding with the atmosphere above the magnetic pole. To us earthlings they appear as shimmering curtains of light, the visible fallout of space storms. They are most brilliant when the sun is the most restless, in periods of greatest sunspots.

Here in the far north this brilliant viewing is possible because of a clear unpolluted atmosphere and long periods of darkness. In winter they have as much as 22 hours out of the 24 without any daylight, not even "twilight." As the sun is not seen from the middle of November until well into January, this is an ideal location for studying the phenomenon. Today the city of Tromso, at the 70th parallel, has one of the world's best planetariums (the Northern Lights Planetarium). Here are shown films, stellar projections, and celestial wonders on a 360-degree screen beneath the building's dome.

How welcome these lights must be during the long dark days of winter, reflecting off white snow. We, who live in northern United States away from lights, have had pleasure in observing these lights in the northern sky, though I'm sure ours can't compare with theirs. In Norway, friends have told me, that as children they were often warned never to whistle at the Northern Lights or they would risk being taken up by them.

Heavy industries, with resulting pollution, are far away, providing unspoiled natural surroundings. Real tranquility is all around, as one walks on the many paths through mountains. Or you can ride a bicycle on wooded trails. Real nature is never far away. The scenery is so beautiful. Tourists, who are lucky with the weather, go home with unforgettable memories.

Besides being one of the world's most beautiful areas, North Norway's coastal area is unique in another way. It is the world's only area above the Arctic Circle that is as well populated and where agriculture is carried on to such a degree.

It was from here, nearly 200 miles above the Arctic Circle near the 69th parallel, that many of Grantsburg's earliest settlers came. Early in the 1860's families there were having difficult times. Farms had been divided over so many generations they were too small to support families, which in some cases were very large. In the mid-1860's there were crop failures, when some folks found it necessary to butcher their livestock for food. Jobs were hard to find and there were many young men looking for opportunities.

Three areas near this latitude contributed to early immigration to the Grantsburg area. One was on Solberg Fjord's coastline, scene of my maternal roots, which I shall refer to as the Coastal Area, or Senja Island. The second is about thirty miles inland, in a valley called Bardu. The third area, Hadsel, I have never visited, but am including information on the many people from there as they made important contributions to early Grantsburg history. Hadsel is an island near the Lofoten area, 235 Norwegian miles from Bardu and well over 150 miles north of the Arctic Circle. It has much in common with the other two areas as far as climate and living conditions go.

Several people came to Grantsburg from Hadsel in the 1860's and one account said Martin B. Johnson and others came to America with Bersvend Thoreson in 1860, but information is limited. Some sources say Peter Skamfer Anderson may have come here one year before the Bardu group. He was from Hadsel (Hadseloy) Island. I would like to share what I have learned about these three areas with the descendents of those who came to Grantsburg in its early years.

If you look at the globe, you find this 69th line of latitude going through Alaska, Northern Canada, and Greenland; through a small part of northern Sweden and Finland, and a long length of Siberia in Russia. None support life, as does this area in Norway. Why? It is due to two factors: (1) the Gulf Stream and (2) the westerly winds. Were it not for their influence, the area would have tundra, permafrost and short summers. The latter it does have, but tundra and permafrost it does not, something they would surely have without the Gulf Stream.

This warming effect of the Gulf Stream is felt all along the coast. For example, at the 69th parallel there is no winter skating on the seawater bordering their land. Salt water in motion and an average January coastal temperature of 25 degrees F. don't permit extensive freezing. On fjords that extend far inland this might not be true. Salty water has presumably been diluted by fresh water pouring down from mountain streams. A tempering effect of ocean winds becomes less as they travel inland, meaning lower temperatures.

The Gulf Stream is a warm ocean current that comes from the Gulf of Mexico, flows across the Atlantic, and then follows Norway's western shores northward. Along with this influence, the area lies in the path of westerly winds, so warmed ocean air is carried inland, making the land a green belt well up into the north. Many of Norway's islands are along this western shore. These islands also act as a "wall," tempering the effect of wild winter storms in land. Surrounded by warmed waters, even some of the Lofotens Islands above the Arctic Circle have almost no frost in winter, making them fine pasturelands.

Westerly winds carry moisture-laden air over the land. As it passes over the mountains, it cools and drops rain or snow on mountainsides much of the year. As the rain falls and the snow melts, many streams with numberless waterfalls carry great quantities of water to the ocean.

This abundance of falling water continues to be a great asset to Norway. Before other power was available, waterfalls ran gristmills that ground grain into flour. Timbers were sawed into building materials and for other uses. Today Norway has more hydroelectric power per person than any other country. It is said only a fifth of the potential is harnessed. Due to this abundance, manufacturing industries are now providing a job market that Norway once did not have. A few of these industries are food processing, wood products, pulp and paper, chemicals, minerals, and others.

One of the more interesting changes is that brought to the fishing industry. The first time I went to Norway I saw many fish drying racks or frames. They were all along the coast. Factories are now processing some of the fish, which are being canned, frozen or dried, and sent all over the world. Cod liver oil is manufactured, and other uses have been found for fish products.

If this is the land of your ancestors, I want to emphasize again how beautiful it is. Its concentration of mountains covers so much of the country you are never out of sight of them. It is a vast area of unspoiled beauty, with mountains rising from the sea in breathtaking formations. Waterfalls cascade down into emerald waters of the fjords. Countless awesome peaks seem to rise out of the ocean, making those 19,000 and more islands Norway is said to have. Mountains and fjords are found almost the entire length of Norway's coast.

Along the coast and in the fjords you see few towns of any size for there is little land suitable for farms and buildings. Mountains often rise right out of the sea. Wherever there is a flat area near the water's edge, there are farms or clusters of homes. Sometimes you can see a working farm clamped securely to a mountainside, so scarce is land for farms or home sites. These mountains are green with trees, mostly pine and birch, or are simply grass covered. Some are just steep rocks with no sign of plants or human life. Farther north, more of the peaks become snow covered.

IV
THE CHANGE OF SEASONS

Summer comes fast to North Norway, when it does finally come. Not with 80 degree temperatures and ripening strawberries, but really welcome longer days of sunlight. Someone wrote me from there on April 13th. The sun was rising at 4:52 AM and setting at 8:40 PM. Each day was lengthening about ten minutes from the previous day, making daylight of the week seventy minutes longer than the last one. By May 24th they have 24 hours of sunlight and can observe the sun each clear night until July 24th at the 69th Parallel.

To understand why this happens we must remember two things. (1) The earth turns on its axis every 24 hours. The equator divides the earth into the two hemispheres, north and south, with the North Pole being the north end of the axis and the South Pole the south end. The earth is tilted on its axis at an angle of 23½ degrees.

Fact (2) the earth revolves around the sun, which is stationary. It takes 365.25 days (leap year 366) to make a complete revolution around the sun. Daytime depends on which side of the earth is exposed to the sun.

Due to the earth's tilt on its axis, at one point half of the earth is exposed to the sun with the poles right on the edge of the dark and light or the sunlit area. This occurs two times on the earth's course around the sun, on March 21st, the vernal equinox and September 21st, the autumnal equinox. The sun is directly over the equator on these days and rises at 6 AM and sets at 6 PM all over the world. (Times given are approximate due to times zones).

In Northern Norway days begin to lengthen much more rapidly than they do for us, for the sun's path is longer. Each day the sunrise and sunset are much farther north and are doing so, so rapidly that by May 24th at midnight, it is still above the horizon at the true north and begins to rise again. It doesn't disappear below the horizon again until about July 24th. In other words there are 24 hours of sunlight for about two months at the 69th parallel. From May 24th until June 21st the sun is higher in the north each midnight. Then it begins to lower until July 24th, when it dips below the horizon as it makes its circle in the sky. From then it disappears farther south and is below the horizon longer, until September 21, when it is back to rising and setting at 6 o'clock just as it did in March, and days are again 12 hours long all over the earth.

Now the days begin to shorten very fast for our friends in the north. On November 24th they watch it just peek over the southern horizon. From then on they will be looking for that January day when even schools might close to celebrate return of the sun.

It is said there are two months of total darkness, but they tell me that is not really so. There is the twilight effect such as we get just after the sunset, and so when the sun is not far below the horizon, there is some light. If it is a clear day and a mountain is not too close, there is enough light to read outdoors at noontime even in December. However if it is cloudy or snowing, lamps have to be lighted all day.

But during these two months of darkness it is really not totally dark. Besides the period of twilight, there are starlight and moonlight on clear days and nights. There are Northern Lights with their brilliant colors being at their best this time of year. It has been calculated that 1440 hours of direct light from the Midnight Sun, daylight during the rest of the year, plus moonlight, starlight and Northern Lights, all produce more total light than is enjoyed at the equator.

V
SILDVIK AND SENJA ISLAND

My first visit to Sildvik was in 1956. Sildvik is in a "vik" or cove on Solberg Fjord. Mountains rise behind it on three sides. A road that followed the sea into the cove with its dozen homes ended there, for the mountain on the western side extended out into the sea. Today a tunnel allows the road to continue through the mountain and south along the shore of Solberg Fjord.

Sildvik looks out across the fjord to Senja Island, where my maternal Grandfather was born. I was rowed across the fjord to the spot where the home had stood, in a real fjord boat with two people rowing. It was maybe a couple of miles or more.

The house had stood close to the mountain that rose close to shore. It must have been well protected from fierce gales that blow off the North Sea. Remnants of a stone foundation were all that remained. Later I was taken to the spot where the cottage was moved. But again all that remained were foundation stones.

All houses in Sildvik face Solberg Fjord to the north, so they can observe sea traffic on its way to and from the North Cape. They can also see the narrow passageway between Senja Island and the mainland. A bridge leading from Finnsnes to Senja now spans this corridor. Finnsnes is the nearest port and town of any size in the area.

They see the Hurtigruten (coastal express) that travels between Bergen and Kirkenes to the far north. One of these ships is leaving each of the two points every day so there are a total of 11 different ships. Thirty-four ports are visited, where freight is delivered, more freight picked up, and passengers get on or off. Every day both southbound and north-bound ships make stops at each designated port. For a long time these boats were the only contact many coastal communities had with the out-side world. They brought mail and freight, and carried passengers to and from coastal ports.

Today passengers are carried on each of the 11 ships. This journey up or down the coast is said to be the "World's Most Beautiful Sea Voy-age." The round trip from Bergen to Kirkenes is 2,500 nautical miles and lasts 11 full days. It is best taken in Midsummer when you can choose waking hours. Sometimes you can wander through a town where a longer stop is made. Gazing at some of the world's most varied and scenic mountain scenery makes it difficult choosing a time to sleep. Accommo-dations on this popular voyage are very good, making early registration necessary.

In the late 1800's one of my grandfather's sisters went across the fjord from Senja to Sildvik to marry a man whose family "farm" was there. The family had three sons and apparently the land was divided among them, as they lived close to one another. Reidar Thomassen was the son of one, and his mother had come from Bardu Valley. In fact two of the brothers had married girls from Bardu.

Each farm had a barn, and two or three cows came down off the mountain every morning and evening to be milked. The next time I vis-ited, in 1972, milk came in cartons. A small plot next to the driveway was planted to potatoes. I measured the plants and found they grew over an inch a day—from two inches to more than eight in the six days we were there—due to the 24 hours of daylight. There were almost no level spots, just a tiny garden, but up the mountain there was a small field. Next to the house there was one of those cascading mountain streams making wonderful music.

Apparently in earlier days these coastal families made their living from the land and the sea. Now all has changed. Many barns stand empty, and except where farmers have acquired more land, few are farming.

Present day industries and means of transportation make them no longer dependent on land or sea.

Anna Rebecca's Move To Sildvik

This is about my Great-grandmother, Anna Rebecca. She was living on Grassmyra, name of the home on Senja Island, where Clement moved the cottage that Grandpa Clementson was likely born in. At least it is, as I understood it when I visited the spot. Ragna (Kristianna's daughter) told this story to Reidar.

In the fall of 1893 or 1894, Kristianna and her husband rowed over the fjord from Sildvik to Grassmyra to visit her mother who was 72 years old. When they were going to row back again, Anna Rebecca insisted on going with them. Both Kristianna and Thomas thought it was too cold for her to sit in the open boat for such a long way (miles). But Anna Rebecca wouldn't give in and said she had her own bed clothes that she could take with her and lay around her if she got cold. "I'm only going to visit," she said. Both Kristianna and Thomas didn't think they should forbid her to come but when they had rowed a long way out, she turned and said, "You don't need to think that I'm going back to Grassmyra." Her husband, Clement, had been in Finnmark for many years. He had left when the children were little and never had been heard from. She stayed in Sildvik for ten years or until she died.

EARLY KLAUVA ON SENJA ISLAND

Senja Island is the second largest island of Norway, situated off the western shore above the Arctic Circle. Most early settlements of Norway's Arctic areas, were along the shore, where Gulf Stream warming was felt.

It was on the Eastern Shore of Senja Island that our Grandfather, Adolph Clementson, son of Clement Johannson, was born and raised. The main source of income for area residents was fishing. Perhaps as far back as the 1600's, a small trading center called Klauva had grown up on the Eastern Shore of Senja Island. Today the small settlement of Sildvik is directly across Solberg Fjord, which separates Senja from the mainland. There is no longer a settlement at Klauva, but the part it played in early area history is remembered.

Gudrun Myrvang Thomassen contributed the following story about Klauva.

There had been trading in Klauva before 1800, but the first well-known merchant was Lorentz Peter Jessen, who came to Klauva in 1807 from Hammerfest, which is farther north in Finnmark.

Jessen took over Klauva after a poor merchant, who at one time had been very rich. In reality it was a merchant in Trondheim, Vogelsang, who bought Klauva this time. Jessen was to look after this trading post for him. Jessen was a clever man and was also an officer in the sea defense of the coast. He was always well dressed, and made a stylish appearance when he came in his black uniform with golden braid, shining buttons and so on. He had a very fine ship and when he arrived in Tromso the whole town bowed to him. In comparison to other merchants, he was a very good man. He helped the people when war came. He gave them credit so they could buy grain for food.

After some years Jessen became owner of this place. He also had an inn where people could sleep and buy food, and he sold "spirits." A man, Leopold von Buch, wrote in 1807 that 300 boats and 1400-1500 people passed Klauva on their way to the Lofotens for fishing. Many of them slept in Klauva every year when they passed the town; so much money changed hands there. Here they could buy what they needed for fishing. The fishermen sold their fish to Jessen, and Klauva was a good harbor, too.

Most of the houses that we can see in old pictures were built when Jessen lived there. People were poor and worked hard at that time. There was a great difference in the living standards of people then. The merchant and priest lived in affluence, but people accepted it; perhaps many believed that it was God's will. Some lived in abundance while some nearly starved.

Jessen's wife "knew who she was." She was well dressed, had a fine house and many servants at her bidding.

One midsummer night they had a party out of doors and many guests were there. A Laplander, (Sami) in a little boat, passed by and Jessen shouted that he must come and get some wine. Jessen gave him the whole bottle and the Laplander was very surprised. The sister of the priest's wife asked if he could "predict" them (tell their fortune). Mrs. Jessen asked, "Would you 'predict' me?" The Laplander, Anders, looked at her for a long time, took her white hand in his and said, "Now you are like the rich man and I'm like Lazarus. But one day you'll become poor. The richness is not of this world, and it will not last long." Mrs. Jessen became quiet and looked down, but then she threw her head back and smiled a mocking smile and said, "And that you believe, Laplander Anders?" Then she took from her finger a broad golden ring and said,

"Look at this ring. It is of more worth than it looks. But this I do." And she threw the ring out over the sea as far as she could. The sea was very deep near the land there, so nobody could find it. Anders was shocked, but she stood there smiling with her long hair down her back and said, *"It is as impossible that the ring can come back as that I can be poor."*

The next day a fisherman came to Klauva with some codfish that he had taken near land. When he gutted one of the fish he discovered a sharp edge on the fish's stomach. He took his knife and opened it. Then a golden ring rolled out on the quay. They sent for Mrs. Jessen and she came down. She stopped, looked at the ring and grew pale. Then she threw her shawl over her face and ran up to the mansion.

Mr. and Mrs. Jessen were the owners of Klauva for only seven years. In 1822 they were bankrupt. They had lived too splendidly, had a great private ship, great houses, many servants. They left Klauva and settled in Solberg not far away. He died a poor man in 1837. His wife lived for many years after him.

One of Jessen's men, Larentz Ovre, was allowed to manage all things there. He also came from Hammerfest. After some years he married Jessen's only daughter.

But a very rich and clever merchant came from Trondheim and was interested in Klauva. He had a splendid ship and he managed to get the place after some years. His name was Knut Moe. Ovre gave up, took his wife with him and settled in Gibostad, on Senja, about 40 km. from Klauva, and had a shop there.

From then (1832) the Moe family ruled Klauva for 70 years. All was built up before so he had only to take over houses, seahouses, stockhouses, animals, servants, and all things. He had about 20 servants. Moe was a chairman in the land council, too, so he had much power. Years went on and he became an old man. His son, Jacob Moe, took over. He was the first man in the land council here in Sorreisa when it became a corporation in 1886.

Even in death they could not mix with the poor. The church consecrated a churchyard for the family there.

Jacob Moe was 12 years old when he came to Klauva. He died in 1892 (73 years old). His son Carl Moe was the next. He died far from Klauva in 1950, but his cinerary urn is placed in the family churchyard.

In the old days the sea was the highway. When roads were built, merchants settled in other places. People do not come to Klauva now. The fairytale is over.

Reidar's story of the experience of a servant girl from Klauva follows:

I think that your Grandfather's father must have been quite poor, since your grandfather's sister Kristianna, had to go to work at 13. During the summer and autumn she was a kitchen servant at Klauva. Klauva is the headland that can be seen across the fjord from Sildvik. At that time Klauva was an important trading center. As a grandmother, she related how the cooks prepared a "soup" of blueberry juice for the merchant and his family. The servants were not served this kind of "soup," but they wanted so badly to taste it that they licked the soup plates after they carried them out of the dining room where the gentry dined.

Even if the people were poor, they managed to subsist if they had a boat, fishing tackle with a hook and silk thread. If they had a mast and a sail on the boat they were in still better circumstances, for then they could reach more distant locations for better fishing.

Reidar Thommasen wrote this portion about Klauva:

The general store at Klauva stood between five or six houses outside of a big boat landing or dock. The main building had two stories plus a loft or attic. In this building were two chimneys or two open fireplaces. Also in the town was a fish store with three boats. They bought and caught fish and took them to Bergen in far south Norway. It was on one of these trips from Bergen, Clement Johannsen came from Bergen and here he met and married Anna Rebecca Thomassen who was employed there at the time. They were Adolph Martin Clementson's parents.

The town was liquidated before or after World War I but many stories are still told of things that happened there. One follows:

Historians tell that at one time a fisherman had stolen a sack of flour and carried it to what was the landing, but it was too far for him to lower it down in his boat. As he was trying to load the sack, Old Mo, the storeowner himself came walking along the dock and when the fisherman saw him said, "This won't go." "Yes, just wait," said Old Mo. "Go down in the boat and take a hold and I'll drop the sack down." He thought the fisherman had bought the flour.

They said Old Mo could neither read nor write. One time a man bought a grindstone that he had charged. Old Mo drew a circle in his book but forgot to draw a hole so when the man came to pay for it, Mo charged him for a cheese instead of a grindstone.

EARLY DAYS IN NORTH NORWAY

Early farms in Norway were first settled in the south where little scattered groups built homes and farms. There they found the broad flat lands, so rare in Norway. These were near present day Stavanger and to the east. This is where Norway's best arable land is found. Webster states that arable land is land suitable for plowing and raising crops. With a small percentage of Norway's land said to be arable (one statement said three percent), one can see why even the smallest piece of good soil is prized in this North Country.

As the years went by and the population grew, these people went farther north and up the West Coast looking for farmlands and a place to build a home. Many fjords along the coast offered miles of shore. In many places mountains rose abruptly from the water but there was usually some fairly level good land between the water and the foot of the mountain. This is where small farms were found all the way up the coast well beyond Tromso to the north.

They also built farms well up the sides of mountains. All along Norway's coast, people looked for hanging valleys or for narrow shelves when farm sites became scarce. Some were even 1200 feet above sea level. Every bit of soil had to be utilized if people were not to starve.

Farming and fishing seemed to be the ways to make a living. For most, the two were combined.

The houses they built were small because they had to be built with material on hand. Therefore there were many small houses in North Norway. The smallest had only one room but the roomiest had both a living room and kitchen on the first floor. Then they had room up over the kitchen where the parents and younger children slept. In the other room that could reach over half the house older children slept until they grew up and the boys could divide a room for themselves. These small houses had no hall or entry room. A cellar was dug under the house. There was always dirt up against the foundation wall to keep grass growing to make a good tight insulation. These preservation cellars were warm and frost-free. Houses were built of round timbers. Wide boards an inch or more thick were laid on the roof. On top of these, birch bark and sod were placed. I think your Grandfather, Adolph Clementson, grew up in a good house that his father, Clement Johannsen had built for himself and Anna Rebecca.

Before 1880 there were few houses that had a stove to cook food on. They had open fireplaces or pits. In the pit they laid a thick slab (better called hearthstone) *set in mortar. Rods were set in such a way that a kettle could be hung in it and raised or lowered according to the size of the flame. When they got their first stove it was set right in the fireplace, but it wasn't too many years before it was taken down. Then they put a new stovepipe in place of the fireplace.*

I heard of one house roof where turf from a lingonberry patch was laid. The wife was able to serve newly picked lingonberries three weeks before they were ripe in other places. One time there were so many berries on a house roof that they picked 20 baskets late in summer and fall. I do not know if this is true but lingonberries have been found growing on roofs of mountain cabins.

Houses up to the 1920's were often of unpainted logs. Some had tar spread on the outside, others not. Sometimes the insides were painted white. When people started to finish insides of houses, they put boards directly on the log walls. Some hung old newspapers on walls for insulation, so if you tore down one of these houses you would find papers 100 years old. Floors were plain boards. The loft was seldom finished under the roof. Rafters might be painted.

Today's homes are as modern as ours. People are as well educated as any in the world, so are aware of what is available. Economical electric power is at hand almost everywhere, so operation of modern devices is no problem.

When I visited there in 1956 that was not true. One thing I remember so well was the living room heating stove which was not being used as it was around July first. The tall fire chamber was a beautiful slender cylinder perhaps a foot across covered with beautiful colored tile. The frame on which it stood and the top were of ornate metal. It burned wood. When I came back in 1972 the kitchen was modern, with stainless steel sinks, refrigeration, electric stove and running water. They perhaps had running water in 1956, because a mountain stream tumbled down to the sea not far from the kitchen door.

About 1900 or before, there were no washing machines or even wash boards. Folks then washed clothes on a specially prepared board. In the spring or summer they went to the river or brook and lay clothes on a rock or a board and beat them with a wooden paddle until clean. The paddle was prepared from a board about 20 inches long and four inches wide. Thickness varied from 1 to 1 ½ inches. At one end it was rounded to form a handle. When they had paddled on one side of the garment, it was turned and the other side paddled. This was repeated several times. But if the garment was extra dirty, the paddle edge was used and even the thumbnail was brought into use. In the spring white clothes or household linens were spread on the snow to bleach.

There was not much variety in food that could be prepared. A coarse mush was made of a mixture of oats and barley meal. Grain kernels were often only cracked. This mush and salt herring were important parts of their winter diet. One told of a "sour soup" made of whey or sour milk with meal or flour for thickening and then boiled. There might be such a shortage of hay for cows in winter that they gave little milk, thus limiting diets still more. Cheese and butter were saved from that produced in the summer months.

Other foods stored for winter were flatbrod, smoked lamb, berries from the woods and mountains and, of course, fish. A common means of preserving some of these was in salt brine in large barrels.

Providing clothing for a family in early years was a real problem, particularly in the more isolated areas. One immigrant told of what he wore when he was a boy. His breeches were made of sheepskin with the wool turned in. His socks were knit of sheep's wool yarn and came above his knees. His shirt and coat were knit or were of cloth woven of wool yarn. In the short summer everyone went barefooted, but when shoes were worn they were carved from wood. Wooden shoes were not practical in the mountains, so moccasin-like shoes were made of cowhide with hair on the outside. Only material at hand was there for them to use.

When a farmer became too old or unable to carry on farm work, he followed a time-honored system of giving the farm to his oldest son, a system known as "kaar." The understanding was that he and his wife would be furnished with necessities of life as long as they lived. In this he developed his own Social Security.

No doubt there were no documents involved in Norway, but only a general understanding. When they came to America, many thought it should be with legal documents. Here in Grantsburg there was a case where a son-in-law had papers drawn so that when they took over her parents' farm, they did just such a thing. Items in the contract give a good idea of what was involved. The document is on record in the Burnett County Court House. Eliminating legal language, items agreed to were:

For the 80 acres (legal description given) for $200 payment he binds self and heirs, that during the couple's lifetime, they promise to provide and care for the old folks, who could continue to occupy the west end of the dwelling, a space of 12x16 feet. In addition they agree to furnish and deliver each year these items:

Two cows and two sheep

Food for these animals

Four barrels of good pure wheat flour

$20 each year

Use of a horse to go to church or any other place as requested

Furnish all firewood needed free of charge

It was then duly witnessed and signed by all parties. This gives us an idea of what was involved in passing property from one generation to another. In some cases the farm was large enough to divide among several children. After a few generations, however, the land was divided into such small farms, many were unable to support a large family. The only employment except for fishing, that often supplemented farming, was for sons and daughters to hire out as servants (tjeners). Wealthier farmers, or those with larger farms, able to produce more food, seemed willing to take them in. One farm might have as many as five or six servants.

The pay was modest. In one area, for a year's work, a servant girl received two pairs of shoes, one dress, two bodices, one skirt, three undergarments, three or four dollars and enough wool to produce two pairs of stockings. A boy or man received one coat, two pairs of shoes, two shirts, one pair of pantaloons, one pair of stockings, two pairs of socks and $10 a year.

Real money was rare and highly valued if you lived far from the sea. This included people far up in the mountains as well as those living inland. They had little to sell, and if they did it was difficult getting to market. Few things did they buy. Most had a hard time getting enough to eat.

On the coast there were more people with money to spend. A ready market was there for easily obtained fish. This explains why men were willing to endure hardships and dangers of long cold months in the Lofotens. I was told that because of these hardships my grandfather at 17 was willing to face the risks of coming to America. He always loved to fish in Wisconsin lakes however.

One immigrant told how his family, who lived on a fjord, gathered "city wood" when he was a boy. This was back in the 1860's, when wood was still the main fuel for heating homes. He and his father went up the mountainside and gathered firewood to bring down to the shoreline. When enough was gathered, his father sold it to a boat owner, who took it to Bergen to be sold as firewood, hence the name "city wood." Later they spent the winter gathering this wood. In the spring his father hired a large sailboat which they loaded with wood. He went along to Bergen, where the wood was sold before they sailed home again. He was really impressed with the things of the big city.

VIII
MOUNTAIN FARMS

For the son who wanted a home and family, he often had to turn to the mountains for a possible farm site, a shelf of land or a tiny valley. These plots of soil were cleared of trees and a home and barn were built for a mountain farm, the solution for many. When areas were very crowded they even turned to a seter far up in the mountains for living quarters.

Many of these farms had to survive as a unit. Often they were very isolated, especially in winter, with no roads or near neighbors. A path led down to the fjord where a rowboat was kept. It could be used for fishing or to row to one of the few area stores for needed supplies. Seldom was there a doctor who could be reached.

Fire that would destroy a home or barn of these widely scattered farms was a constant threat. Of course, there were no organized fire departments, and by the time neighbors noticed the fire and help arrived, destruction was complete, with little saved. However, neighbors from near and far arrived to help with building a new home, cutting timbers for walls, peeling birch bark and digging turf for roofing. Food was brought, and they worked long hours. Every effort was made to have a home built before arrival of winter if the fire happened that time of the year.

There was little communication with the outside world. Contacts with others were made by foot or by a hand-rowed boat on the fjord. Young men looking for a mate had limited choice. No farm could carry on without both a woman and a man to do the work. When a young wife died and left the husband with little children, he might marry a much older woman in order to survive as a family. Young men might marry women in their forties or fifties.

Once buildings were ready, the soil was prepared for planting. Potatoes and cabbage were two vegetables that grew well at this latitude. They were planted about May first. Potatoes had reached Norway from the Americas by way of Europe as recently as the 1750's. Barley, oats and wheat were grains commonly grown. It was always a constant struggle to get enough to eat, to supplement fish that were plentiful in streams and fjords.

Each farm kept a cow or two for milk, cheese and butter, important items in their diet. Sheep were kept for wool, so necessary for their clothes. It was the only available material for clothing, unless they used hides of wild animals or from their sheep. Even birch bark was used for shoe soles, etc. Lambs or cattle were butchered for meat in their diet.

Grass was a very precious commodity for a Norwegian farmer to feed his animals in the summer, as well as eight darker months when snow covered the ground and animals were kept inside barns. Grass that grew around farm buildings was cut with a scythe, dried on wires strung between posts, and later stored in the barn loft. Animals were taken up in the mountains to graze as soon as grass began to turn green, well into May.

Grandpa's Story

Here is a story Reidar's grandfather told him: *"We were three boys who herded livestock in the mountains in summer; my brother Hans, 8 years old, myself 10 years and a neighbor boy my age. One summer we had a ram (sheep) that attacked us whenever we turned our backs.*

One warm day we gathered all the animals together in a small opening in the woods on the shore of a small tarn (mountain lake). Because of the heat we took off our dungaree blouses (tunics) and hung them on a stump at the water's edge and then began to pick blueberries at the edge of the woods. Sheep came grazing along the shore and when this ram caught sight of our tunics he thought it was one of us. He immedi-

ately took an offensive stance, gathered himself for a spring, and like a cannonball sped directly to the stump. There was a sound of a break as the stump gave way and a splash as the ram hurtled headfirst into the water. We had to help him get back on land. Exhausted, the ram slunk away into the woods and lay down. After that he never troubled us again."

During late summer much time was spent in the mountains harvesting grass wherever it grew. It was gathered in bundles after it had dried on wires, and carried down to the barn, or hauled home later by sleigh when needed in winter. If roads were not available it was carried home on a cart or in a sack on someone's back. Some years there was a lack of rain, resulting in a hay shortage. Then all family members scrounged for every blade of grass or gathered twigs of birch trees or juniper, something our deer resort to for winter feed. Sometimes cattle were so weak by spring from lack of food they had to be carried out of the barn, or so the stories tell. Likely they were fed a near starvation diet, to make the hay last. Cows weren't expected to produce much milk during the winter.

Most farms had seters in early days. These were summer pastures in the mountains—sometimes many difficult miles to reach—maybe even up to the tree line. Livestock were driven up sometime after June first when that grass was beginning to green. There might be snow patches to wade over, high mountains to cross and rivers to ford. Then around the middle of September, hopefully before the first snow, they were brought down again. Cheese and butter were made at the seter during these summer months.

Occasionally the seter was so close to the farm those maids could go up in late afternoon to milk the cows and spend the night. The next morning they again milked the cows and carried milk down to the farm in wooden buckets hung on yokes. There it was made into cheese and butter.

In late summer other family members brought up the scythe and rakes and gathered hay for a long winter. The seter was a place to enjoy long days of sunshine for those living above the Arctic Circle under the Midnight Sun.

Today you might visit a seter, but it would likely not be a "working seter." Instead they might be quarters for tourists who like hiking in the mountains. Well-marked mountain trails can be followed to find these accommodations and many do, as they choose to enjoy the unspoiled beauty of this far North Country.

IX
WE VISIT A SETER

Each day the sun's rays become more powerful and it melts snow that they can expect into May. As soon as the snow is melting, grass will begin to grow and it is time to take sheep and cattle to the mountains. Every blade of grass near the farmyard must be saved to feed livestock over the long eight-month winter.

Plants grow at an unbelievable rate when the sun shines for 24 hours. There is one plant, the Tromso Palm, which has been known to grow up to four feet in 24 hours and about 14 feet in two months. This is too much for it, so it withers.

If the farm has a seter in the mountains, cattle must be brought up there the last of May or the first part of June, where they must feed for the summer. A seter is a summer pasture well up into the mountain where animals live during the short summer. It is equipped with a building to shelter milkmaids, who must care for the cattle and make cheese and butter from cows' milk. Summer is the period of their greatest production.

Seter buildings were built of materials available nearby. Often they were made of stones or timbers. The roof was of small logs and covered with birch bark and turf so grass and flowers often grew on it. Likely there was a crude fireplace for heating and cooking, with a crude crane built to hold cooking kettles. There was no oven for baking bread. With cattle feeding in the seter, grass for hay grew down on the farm for feeding during the long winter.

Lucky were those who had a horse to draw the load of equipment and supplies on a difficult journey. Included were a churn, kettles for butter and cheese making, wooden milk pails, cheese molds, cups and plates, knives and spoons, a frying pan, coffee kettle and other things. Then there was salt for the cattle, flour to mix with whey for the calves, coffee and sugar. The milkmaids packed their supplies, bedding, and Sunday clothes as well as their work clothes. They brought yarn to knit, cloth to embroider, and other things, for they spent the summer up there.

Now they are off for the long hard climb over snow banks and going up and down mountains to get to the summer home of the milkmaids and the cows' summer pasture. Once they arrived at the seter, equipment was stored away in the seter building. Growing grass was found for cows to feed on, for they were hungry after their long journey. When all was done, family members started their long trek down the mountain, leaving the milkmaids to milk cows morning and evening, and to turn the milk into butter and cheese. In their leisure time they did knitting and handwork which they brought along.

Girls went for the cows each morning and evening, but often cows came to the seter buildings by themselves. Milk was set out in pans for the cream to rise, skimmed and then churned into butter and put in molds. The milk was made into cheese. Whey from churning was mixed with flour and fed to calves. There were dishes to be washed. These were taken to a nearby stream and scoured with sand and juniper branches, followed by a generous rinsing in clear water.

Most farms had a few goats and they, too, were milked and their milk made into goat's cheese.

Ever so often someone from the farm traveled up to the seter to bring supplies for the milkmaids and to bring down butter and cheese. Or they might stay for a few days and harvest some mountain grasses, which were brought down in the winter to feed the animals. Homefolks weren't the only visitors. Often young swains and other young folks traveled up the mountains to visit the lonesome milkmaids. These visits were most likely to happen on Sunday, when everyone was dressed in his best.

Sometimes maids from other seters joined them.

Down on the farm they prepared for winter. In fact all summer was devoted to storing up supplies.

Their three main endeavors were (1) to store food for the table, (2) to make clothes for their backs, (3) to put hay in the barn.

Many homes had a "stabbu" (small one-room building away from the house). These storage places were often attractively decorated with rosemahling (decorative painting). Grains, butter, cheese, and other foods were stored there for the long winter. Other things were stored there as well. To keep out invading animals, such as bears looking for food, the structures were well off the ground on four sturdy poles. These served to elevate the building well beyond animal reach.

Then there was wood to cut for the long winter. When the grass was ready for hay it was cut with a scythe, hung to dry on long wires and later stored in the hayloft. If the father was a fisherman, there always were fishnets to mend and equipment to ready for winter fishing.

Mother was busy in the storeroom, where her loom had been set up for the warm months. There she wove cloth from yarn she made from sheep's wool. Later the cloth was made into coats and other things for the family.

By the middle of September summer was really over and days were soon shortening fast. It might snow any day. There were the animals and milkmaids to bring down, along with all the supplies. Hay was safely stored in the barn. Potatoes were dug and stored in the cellar. Firewood was neatly piled near the house. Winter was on its way.

Another seter story follows that was told by one who grew up in Norway.

Our family went up to the seter in July. We had four cows, four sheep, eight goats, four chickens, a rooster, pig, dog and cat.

On the way, there were many hills to climb. The cows, sheep and goats were driven up first. Chickens were carried on the back in a sack. Father took a horse-drawn cart with utensils for milking and cheese making as well as other dishes. The pig and cat rode along.

Down on the farm potatoes were already planted and growing but we had to cut grass growing around the seter. We did that early in the morning when it was easier to cut. We cut wood for the fire that was needed to make cheese and fix our meals. Sometimes we cut wood to take down to the farm.

Mother milked cows each morning and night, and made butter and cheese. The children's job was to herd cows during the day, milk the goats, and pick cloudberries and blueberries. They also fished in the mountain lakes.

Sunday was a holy day and no work was done. Friends might come up to the seter to visit if the weather permitted.

We stayed at the seter a month and a half and came down in August. Some trips had been made down to sell cheese besides to bake bread.

There were often Sami herding their reindeer in the higher mountains. We had to chase reindeer from fields where their animals fed. The Sami paid for damages their reindeer did to the seter.

Seters have not been in use for maybe 50 years. Today there are other ways to supplement their income without hard work involved in going to the seter.

X
COASTAL LIFE IN EARLY DAYS

On farms by the coast, life's work was a combination of fishing and farming. People had from one to five cows, from two to ten sheep, some chickens, and the big farms also had a horse. Because mountains often led right down to the water, there was little level land for fields and building spots. Fishing was a big part of life of the coastal people. Thus the farmer supplemented a meager living his small farm supplied, enabling the family to live more comfortably.

The last of January, men left their homes, wives and children to go fishing in the Lofotens, a group of islands to the south. The wife stayed at home in a poor house and in earlier days, without electricity, and many times without wood nearby. Often she had her in-laws living with her. If there were no older people, the wife had to take children with her to the barn until they got old enough to be left alone in the house. Of course, she was used to milking and caring for the cows. (Someone said that as late as 1920 it was considered shameful for a man to milk cows. His sphere was fishing.)

About the last of April men came back from fishing in the Lofotens, and then the wives had to immediately get everything ready for their men to go to Finnmark (to the north) to fish for cod. In the spring it was

40

extra hard for the wife, as there was often a shortage of food for the cattle. She had to cut seaweed (at low tide) that she carried home to the farm on her back. There the seaweed was cooked together with salted heads of fish as well as the roe. These were wastes from the Lofoten fishing that the men brought home. Some farms also cut grass in the mountain woods and fields. Men may not have racked and hauled enough hay home before they left for their Finnmark fishing. It was then the wife got help from a neighbor. She might take a big sack and go early in the morning, often as far as a Norwegian mile (seven English miles). She would either carry the hay, or pull a cart home with hay, in order to keep the cattle alive. This was done until late May or early June. By then grass was growing in the mountains where the cattle were taken to graze.

About this time of the year it began to get warmer, allowing a loom to be set up in the stabbur (storehouse), or if there wasn't any other place, it was put in the barn or hay mow, now that they were empty. There the women wove cloth for both outer and under clothes made from wool of sheep on the farm. This had been washed, carded and spun the previous fall and winter. After the cloth was woven, it was laid in a box and dampened and tramped or stomped on, so the material got tighter and thicker.

The "stomper" was made of two-inch planks and another plank on top. Usually it was four feet wide and six feet long. This wetting and pounding of the material, as well as the length of this treatment, deter-mined quality and thickness of the material. The finest material was used for "going to church" clothes, while the coarser was for work clothes.

The finest material might, in some homes, be made of linen if avail-able. That was used for white goods. Women were often clever at weav-ing designs or figures in the cloth with or without a pattern to follow. (Flax, from which linen is made, was not grown in North Norway.)

A married woman in those days had to be able to do everything. She would card, spin, and weave. She had to be a mother, lover, nurse, doc-tor, housemaid, judge, cook, nursemaid, seamstress, veterinarian, and hay-raking girl. All this she had to be besides being able to pick and can berries, help with butchering and making sausages. And if there was time and there were several neighbors, two of the women could put a boat in the sea and get fresh fish for the table. Other food came from the animals. Some farms were too small to support a cow, so they might have two or three sheep and five or six goats.

XI
THE LOFOTENS AND FISHING

This area is no less beautiful than the rest of the coast. Someone said that scenery on the shore between the cities of Bodo and Tromso was the West Coast's wildest. Here are found the Lofoten Islands. These islands we know as Lofotens include the Vesteraalens to the north and Lofotens to the south. The Hadsel area is one of the islands in the south of the Vesteraalens.

The western walls of these islands abound in the grandeur of jagged mountains with abrupt sides. Higher peaks are snow covered and even small glaciers can be seen in some mountain hollows. Some are more protected, where wild westerly winter winds don't reach, and the view is less rugged. Here there is a variety of scenery where green grass flourishes the year around. Forests or ferns and moss cover the mountains. Some have sheltered spots with rich soil where small farms are found. Flavorful strawberries are even grown on Senja and Kvaefjord Islands, where they ripen under the sun's long days in August.

In sheltered nooks, where bare rocks at the base of mountains reflect heat of the sun's rays, daisies have been known to bloom on April 7. Where but in such a place at this latitude, favored by the Gulf Stream, could such happen? It is said that the islands in places seldom have freezing temperatures though they lie well above the Arctic Circle.

As more settlers moved up the coast they looked to Lofoten fishing for a source of income. Fisheries have always played an important part in the economy of organized Norway. Much of this activity took place in the Lofoten Islands. Being one of ocean fishing's most productive areas in the world, it was a leading source of income for Norway until that began to change following World War I.

Since the days of Vikings, Lofoten Islands have been known for their cod fishing grounds. In Viking times they were scenes of much activity, for it was in the coastal areas that the Vikings' famous ship building developed. Their boats, with ease of sailing as well as rowing, made it possible to carry on as traveling traders and to do their pillaging and colonizing. Boats have always been essential to life on these Norwegian shores. For years the sea was their only highway.

Lofotens are the setting of Edgar Allen Poe's tale "Descent Into The Maelstrom," inspired by the Moskenes whirlpool found off the islands. This takes place where powerful tidal currents form a dangerous whirlpool. Many ships have been caught in this whirlpool and destroyed. Four times a day immense quantities of water, moved by tides, enter and leave the narrow passage, causing the whirling waters. There are others but few as strong as the one Poe made so famous. Areas around these "maelstroms" make excellent fishing grounds.

This group of islands is located well above the Arctic Circle. They lie between 67 and 69 degrees north latitude. Here one would expect a climate like that of northern seaside Alaska, which is at similar latitude, but again, thanks to the Gulf Stream, some islands might have few freezing temperatures. Some are so well sheltered they have fine agricultural land, while others have extended forests.

Because of these warmer temperatures, codfish are attracted to them, making these islands one of the world's finest fishing grounds. Codfish have a predictable pattern in their migration. Most of the year they keep to the north in the eastern Arctic Ocean, where they put on fat in preparation for their long swim to the Lofoten Islands. This is where they go for their annual spawning, with warmer waters necessary for a successful hatch. Ideally, cod want water temperatures of 42 to 44 degrees F. for spawning. Though much of the water here is 37 to 39 degrees F., somewhat warmer than waters to the north, the cod are constantly moving

about to find warmer spawning waters. This means fishermen must be moving about looking for best spawning spots. When spawning ceases (near the end of April) the cod return to colder Arctic waters, to put on weight and to achieve full growth for the next Lofoten fishing season.

Cod begin to arrive about the middle of January and so do the fishermen. This was true long before the turn of the century. Lofoten fishing was a very important part in lives of coastal area men of North Norway, including those living on Solberg Fjord near the 69th parallel. They came in their fjord rowboats equipped with small sails and which might have as many as five pairs of oars. There might be a small removable cabin for storage and sleeping. The distance for some was possibly close to 200 miles. The journey might take a week, depending on weather. Winter storms of snow and gale force winds strike frequently. Then, by traveling close to shore, a sheltered spot would likely be found. All this changed as time went on. By 1880 better boats were available, and by 1907 were motorized. Today, with modern boats, the journey can be made in 24 hours.

Each owner's boat might have a crew of family members or men he had hired. Each one had his food supply to supplement fish that would be their main diet. Each had clothes and bedding needed for winter days ahead. Most of these were packed in chests of a size easily handled, perhaps 33 by 20 by 19 inches, such as one I saw in a Norwegian home. Some are in America today where they are someone's cherished memento from the voyage to a new land. It was necessary to carry drinking water for the journey. This might be made of sour whey, mixed with fresh water and stored in barrels.

A fisherman's life was dangerous. In the days of sailboats a sudden winter storm on a dark night could wipe out most of a fishing fleet. Should they be from one area, there would be a settlement without able-bodied men. None had survived. With the coming of motorboats and steamboats, equipped with radios, early warning was possible, making lives of fishermen safer.

XII
PREPARATIONS FOR THE LOFOTENS

Reidar's account of preparations made at the fisherman's home for a stay of two and a half months or more in the Lofotens follows:

We can easily see that preparations for the Lofoten fishing were begun early in the fall, especially those who were going to fish with nets. They had to use their free time to prepare the fishing tackle. By the first of December work was really speeded up. As soon as there was enough snow, the winter wood had to be hauled home. It was sawed, split and piled in neat rows before they set out for fishing.

Besides, new clothing had to be made and old repaired. The wife had to prepare outer and inner clothing. Four or five pairs of large sea mittens and the same number of long stockings and three to four pairs of heavy footlets had to be knitted. After knitting machines came into use, knitted underwear was made on them. But before these machines, the wife had to knit them.

For food, about 20 loaves of "stompbrod" plus lefse and flatbrod, sylte and other kinds of meat were packed. Spreads like butter, jam and cheeses were prepared and put in jars. All were put in a chest (capacity

120 liters or larger). Under the cover there was space for fine clothes and underwear to be stored.

When it came time to leave from home on their fishing trip, last minute things had to be done. In a chest a scissors was placed along with a darning needle, writing paper, a songbook, a testament, silverware and their tackle used for fishing. Their clothes were laid out and food was packed.

Around the turn of the century they used small open boats. One size was from 33 to 36 feet long or it could be 42 to 47 feet. Both sizes were without a deck, with only a little cabin in back that was taken off as soon as they reached the Lofotens.

Let us now dress the fisherman and send him on his way. The night before he is to leave, they carry in water to warm on the stove. After the children have gone to bed, he takes a bath. Maybe the wife helps him wash his hair and beard and scrubs his back or sees that he does a good job of it! Then he puts on his warmest underwear as it can get very cold sitting all day in an open boat. In the morning he stands up and puts long stockings on, puts on thinner outer pants and buttons on his shirt and vest.

Then he puts on homespun pants. On his feet he has put a pair of thick footlets inside his knit socks. After that his jacket goes on with a thick home knit sweater with a tall collar. On his feet he puts a long pair of leather overshoes. On his head he has a fur or knit cap. If the weather is bad and wind blows from the northeast, he wears the best leather pants and sweater.

He goes around in the barn and says goodbye to the animals. There is always the chance he won't get home again. Then he gives the children a big hug, kisses his wife and a last "God Tur" (good trip) is called as he goes down to the ocean.

If there is straw or other things left after him it must not be cleaned up or thrown out that day as it could give him poor fishing luck or maybe worse.

Once they arrived in the chosen fishing area they moved into living quarters, which were small buildings, usually red, built on stilts over the water. Fish buyers also slept there but spent their days working among the fishermen. Today these red buildings are still around but usually used as tourist sleeping quarters. Each day men would go out in their boats to the fishing grounds looking for the best catch. They often used nets or lines and at the end of the day brought in a load of fish to sell to buyers who had larger ships that came from Bergen. Fish the buyers bought were loaded on these boats, where they were cleaned and salted. Wastes from the fish (heads, entrails, etc.) were set aside. When loaded, the ships left for Bergen, where the fish were marketed worldwide.

Some were bought, cleaned, dried on slabs of rocks and salted for Klipp fish (Lutefisk), which was an important ingredient on all genuine Scandinavian Christmas tables. Others were cleaned, and split into two long pieces up to the head. Then they were hung on racks to dry. (This without salt.) The climate of North Norway made air-drying possible. Besides, there are few flies, snakes or mosquitoes. Heads and entrails were packed in barrels and taken home for cattle food. These were cooked with seaweed harvested at low tide. The livestock savored this mixture, when hay was short in late winter

Swindling By Fish Buyers and Others

Fish buyers would trick the fishermen in many different ways. If it was good fishing one day, they paid less than when fishing was poor. Before 1920 they paid per 100 fish. They also had what they called "big 100." That was 120 and they paid a little more than for 100. They could also count 77-78-79 and then start again at 77. Fishermen weren't organized so buyers did as they pleased. What the fisherman didn't sell he threw back into the sea.

Buyers would treat a drink for a fish on Saturday night. Since the boxes stood outside after the fish inside them were counted, any fisherman with a craving for a drink but who had caught no fish could go to these boxes, take a fish and go in to show it to the buyer to get his drink. Thus with a fish he hadn't even caught, he could drink himself good and drunk on one fish.

XIII
APRIL AND THE RETURN HOME

They stayed in the Lofotens' good fishing grounds until the last of April. Now for several days the boats have been with full sail. The sea is rushing so they sail close to the land on the way home.

As they know it is time for the men to return, children, wives and old people go up to the lookout hill to watch to the south for the fathers, friends and sons. When they are sighted, a large group of young people rushes down from the hill yelling a welcome.

Then the men land and everyone gives them a happy greeting. The next day they unload all their fish and big barrels or containers with dried fish heads and with salted roe (fish eggs). This is food for the cattle.

Now the father will be home for a few days before he leaves for Finnmark for more fishing. He has to haul manure out to the fields and if they need more hay he must take a wagon to get it (even working at night). Or else he can get seaweed to feed the cows.

The summer growing season comes late. Plowing starts in May, when snow is gone and frost is out of the ground. Without a plow the men break up the ground with spades. Many places there are a lot of stones so they have made fences out of them, maybe a yard wide and a yard high. *The days it rains they work on their nets either in the kitchen or boathouse.*

In the meantime his wife has washed his clothes, done some baking (maybe some haddock fish cakes) to add to that she did earlier. This creates supplies for him in Finnmark, from where he doesn't return until late June.

While he is gone and as the weather warms, his wife and hired help start cutting grass for hay—if the growing season has come early—and put it on the wires to dry. She has had to plant potatoes and corn (wheat). (It is too far north and summers too short for our ear corn to grow). *Later they cut the grain.*

Meanwhile shippers are now at Finnmark to buy more fish that are taken care of in the same way. Later in the summer all the dried fish are put on a boat and taken to Bergen and sold. On the return trip the shippers have wares for both the shipper's and crew's families and for other people who wanted goods from the south. Often people who wanted to move or travel from one place to another could go with the shippers.

While the men are fishing in Finnmark, fish are cleaned, salted, and put on board the larger boat. When it is loaded, the boat sails back to homes of the fishermen. There the fish are taken on land, washed and laid over stones to dry. These are called "Klippfisk." There the young and old women that couldn't be out fishing, but were doing other work, take care of these fish. When the fish are dried they are stored in a building by the water. (These are food for later use).

But before the hay and grain are all in, the men return for St. Hans Holiday (June 24). The trees are in leaf and with a neighbor's help, the father cuts wood for heating. The stoves, which take little space, are beautiful, tall and slender, with sides of decorated tiles.

Sometimes they find a field of the nicest birch trees, which are cut, and the bark peeled with a special knife. The bark is tied and piled in big bundles. Later they soak the bark in water to be used for shoes and roof tops. Besides these uses the small twigs and branches were sometimes chopped as food for cows.

When the husbands are home from fishing they always find plenty to keep them busy. One thing is preparing the nets for next year's fishing. These nets, as well as the yarn or ropes used to make fishnets, were usually kept in the attic. This room might not be very deep and five or six feet in diameter. If a lot of nets were needed it might take all summer to make them. After that was taken care of, they could rest until the middle of August but often it took until late in September to finish them. By that time the potatoes are dug and brought into the root cellar. Then the hay is brought home from the hillsides. (By sleigh if it has snowed). As soon as the grain, which was mostly wheat, was ready, it was threshed and made into flour.

In September and October the men went to the "drivgarnfiske" (drifting net) and got their sild. They might be away as long as two months. Each household required a barrel of salted herring (sild) to be caught in the fall for winter food. If it was a big household it might require two barrels of herring. This was considered an emergency food.

When it was September the sheep had to be brought home from the mountains. This was because the sheepman (who watched them all summer) had to leave. About a hundred years ago there were a lot of bears and wolves in the North.

To prove this, here are two of Reidar's bear stories:

My Grandmother Kristiana (Reidar's) could have been 10 years old when this happened. They had sheep on a farm and kept them in a rail fence at night. One night a bear came, broke down the fence and killed two sheep. The bigger one was a buck from which the bear tore the testicles, then threw it down in the falls of the creek. In the morning they found the buck with enough life so that they could slaughter it for meat.

A Brave Hunter *(Believe this?)*

This happened in Sildvik, over a hundred years ago, after my grandmother Kristiana moved there. (Sildvik is across from Senja Island. Solberg Fjord separates them.) *Early one morning in September a young bear came down, took a sheep out of the fence and carried it off. My Grandfather's brother, Kristian Thomassen, took out after the bear. About a kilometer from the house he saw the bear again. Kristian was a big man and even if he was weaponless he jumped on the bear and hit him on the head. A fight began between a human and an animal and the human won. The bear was so mad that he sat on the hill and hit his paws together so it echoed in the mountains. But Kristian was back of the bear and it did not dare attack. He walked backward away from the bear, carrying the sheep that was hardly hurt. When he was far enough he turned and chased the sheep home.*

51

XIV
SMORGASBORD OR COLD TABLE

Some say "smorgasbord" is Swedish inspired but that Norwegians have their "koldt bord" (cold table). Basically they are the same except that the "smorgasbords" are more likely to have hot dishes. However here in America "smorgasbord" is the more commonly heard term.

I have vivid memories of examples of these well-laden tables, particularly breakfast tables. These were in better hotels on my first visit to Norway in 1956. Of course they didn't have all these things, but a good variety of them. There were many seafood dishes prepared in a variety of ways, and countless dishes with cheese, such as Swiss, blue, goat, gammelost (strong cheese), and various meat dishes such as meat loaf and sausages. Then there were fruits treated in various ways, fresh, marmalades, sauces, different salads, and of course various kinds of bread including flatbread.

Here are a few of the Norwegian foods most of our older Norwegians are familiar with:

- Lutefisk: lye fish.
- Gammelost: old cheese.

- Rommegrot: porridge of thick sour cream and flour boiled to thicken, and sprinkled with cinnamon and sugar.
- Akevitt: strong liquor of potatoes and caraway seeds.
- Farikal: mutton and cabbage boiled together.
- Fiskekaker: fish cakes made from cod and other fish.
- Lefse: pancakes made from potatoes, milk, butter, sugar and flour.
- Spekeskinke: sweetened and smoked ham with a lot of salt and a little sugar.
- Gravlaks: salmon sprinkled with salt, sugar, pepper and dill; left for 2 or 3 days, turned 2 times a day.

A word about lutefisk or lye fish. It has been termed "a Yuletide atrocity, a taste that can only be experienced and not described." Not all Scandinavians will agree, for there are many who will drive great distances to enjoy lutefisk suppers.

Lutefisk is dried cod prepared in potash lye. In the book, "Of Norwegian Ways" by Vanberg it is told that in three months time, around 1970, the world's largest lutefisk producer located in Minneapolis, Minnesota, had sold more than a million pounds of it. No doubt some of those pounds came to this Scandinavian area.

XV
COMMUNICATIONS

Ships were the leading means of transportation and communication from the time of Vikings for early coastal people, while the sea was their highway. Even much of the local travel was done by boat, for most homes and villages were built along beaches and in harbors. It is said most people lived within a fifteen-minute walk of the water. Trails and footpaths served local communities, some being wide enough to accommodate horse drawn carts.

Everything changed with coming of automobiles in the early 1900s. Faster transportation brought more communication between coastal areas and the interior. This meant there was a need for wider roads, and their upkeep. Things could be brought in and out by trucks instead of all things by boat. No longer were the light houses, buoys and channels the only items needing constant upkeep, but now it was the ferries, bridges and tunnels, all of which were very expensive to build and keep in repair.

Springtime brings the usual problem of frost heaves or boils. There are load limits during this period, which creates a problem for some industries requiring heavy raw materials. Unless enough can be brought in earlier, they might have to close for lack of material. Industries that use timbers may have problems especially if summer is slow in coming.

Most all coastal homes and villages were built near the shoreline because that was where the land was level enough for buildings and with fertile soil to grow food to maintain a couple of cows and some sheep. So, unless homes were built up on mountainsides, they were accessible for water travel.

Most roads are built close to the shoreline on the more level land. Where they are close to water or there is a sharp drop-off, a fence of metal guardrails is built on one side. There are places where a mountain drops abruptly into the sea, so there is no shoreline on which to build a road. Then a tunnel is blasted through the rocks. Where neighbors living on either side of the mountain could only reach each other by boat or by going great distances by land, now it can be done by car in a matter of minutes. Of course tunnels are costly to build, especially the longer ones. Some in the mountain passes are nearly a mile long. There are even road tunnels built 300 feet below the sea, to join islands. Two of these add up to almost a half mile long. There are a total of 530 or more road tunnels in all of Norway.

Norway has thousands of islets besides the 19,000 larger ones, many of which are occupied. Ferries have carried passengers between islands as well as to the mainland for many years. With the coming of automobiles, larger ferries capable of carrying cars and buses as well as passengers were built. Buses have priority and cars line up as they arrive, so in busy seasons this might mean long waits for crossing.

With road building, many bridges had to be built across streams and to join islands with the mainland. In some cases they are quite long, crossing a wide fjord to join an island to the mainland.

Road upkeep is not easy. There are landslides as well as snow slides in the winter. With snow possible from September to May, keeping roads open at all times is difficult. Because there are periods of thawing in winter, especially along the coast, icing can be a problem as well as heavy snowfall. Winter tires with studs help deal with these problems and heavier loads use chains for safer traction. Studded tires or chains cannot be used in North Norway between May 1 and October 15. Some mountain passes have to be closed in the far north but usually it is only temporary. To help keep the surface free of snow, roadbeds are usually built higher than the borders, allowing snow to blow across. Of course, snowplows are always there and snow fences keep some snow from blowing on the roads.

When a mountain road is likely to be closed by a snowstorm a caravan of travelers is formed. The group is then led through the area in question by snowplows. Road personnel are ready to assist anyone in trouble and to see that all get through. Emergency shelters are built into the mountains, where travelers can be cared for comfortably until roads are again open.

There are no trains in North Norway. The closest railroad to take one to the south can be reached by bus at Bodo on the coast or at Fauske in the interior. At Narvik a rail line crosses into Sweden. This was built to give iron mines at Kiruna in Sweden an ice free port for exporting iron. This line goes south to Stockholm. When riding the train to southern Norway, one goes through many tunnels.

XVI

BARDU VALLEY

Now we will go over the mountains from the coastal area and explore the Bardu Valley. There are countless descendents here in America, many in Grantsburg, whose roots are in this beautiful spot. If you are among them, I am attempting to give you a bit of background concerning your ancestors. Bardu Valley is more than twice as long as it is wide, with the river Malselv running through it from south to north. An individual climbed to one of the higher mountains and viewed the valley, saying there were 20 to 30 mountains surrounding it. Fairly level land, of which there is so little in all of Norway, is usually found around rivers and branches. Mountainsides, which rise up from the valley, are usually covered with a growth of timber—fir, spruce and birch—a valuable commodity for the area. Spruce are at lower levels, with birch at 3000 to 3900 feet elevation, while the willow and dwarf birch are above that. Snow can be seen on the higher mountains, some of it being glaciers that are there all year.

Bardu is the only municipality in the county of Troms without a seaboard. Bardufoss in the northern part of the valley has an airport and an army base. The airport was first built in 1937, but during WWII, Germans were in control and enlarged it. The army post has NATO connections and armed forces from other NATO countries come here for training. There is another post nearby at Satermoen. Today these places offer employment to the surrounding area, particularly for their services. Bardu people can commute to the coastal area for employment. At Sorreisa the country's largest radar facilities are found.

These days they have a military exercise called "shong resolves," where every NATO country takes part.

Temperatures here are not as mild as on the coast. Air has to rise over mountains before it reaches the valley. I was told it might be minus five degrees Fahrenheit (minus 20 degrees Centigrade) for a usual temperature in winter. The coldest can be as low as minus 40 degrees Fahrenheit (-40 C). Because the air is dry and there is no strong wind in the valley, minus 40 degrees Fahrenheit doesn't feel as cold as it might. Temperatures on the coast are much milder due to the oceanic influence. However, in summer the valley can get as warm as 70 to 85 degrees Fahrenheit (20 C to 30 C), much warmer than on the coast.

With short summers and thus short growing seasons, trees aren't likely to reach the size they do here. I saw a picture where two pre-teenagers together reached around a tree. This might not impress us. I did measure a log 19 inches in diameter.

The Malselv area, just to the north of Bardu in Troms County, is one of Norway's principal producers of timber. There are nearby industries that use this timber, one being a chip board factory at Sorreisa. One drawback for such industries, however, is that warehouses must be filled with raw materials before spring thaw restrictions go into effect for heavy-load bearing axles.

Bardu River empties into the Malselv, which flows into the ocean. All along these rivers is an unusual acreage of fairly flat land, unusual for North Norway. Mountains rise on all sides and these mountains are used for summer sheep grazing. Because sheep are left to graze over mountainsides, some predators prove to be a menace, just as they were in earlier days.

In the 18th century (1700) Bardu Valley was a remote area to people on the coast, about 30 miles away. The area separating them was a mountainous, forested, uninhabited wilderness. It is hard for us to imagine how difficult it was to travel between the two points. Occasional hunters may have been there because of many wild animals in the mountains.

Open areas were likely pastured by the wandering Sami, but there were no permanent residents. They stayed close to the coast at this latitude.

In the late 1700's two men, Jens Holmbee from Senja and Troms, and Nikolai Romm, a forest inspector, journeyed through the forested valley of Bardu and decided that trees could be cleared in places where both hay and grain could be grown. Thus there was a potential for future farms even though it was in the far north. Word spread that land was available.

In 1783 the government put out word that land could be claimed here in the north. It is told that any individual would be granted all the land that he could run around in one day. Forests and mountains as well as streams must have limited what could be covered in a day. From the size of earlier area farms, this story could be true.

At this period many families to the south were having difficult times. Population was increasing. Farms that had been divided and handed down for generations became so small they were unable to support large families. This was due to the custom of a father dividing his farm among his sons, though in some cases it was given to the oldest son. In either case the parents expected lifetime care in return. There were no job opportunities for young men, so owning a small piece of land would be their only way to make a living. After generations, larger farms had been divided into many small ones. They could not grow food enough for the family and their livestock. Individual farms might harvest no more than 40 pounds of grain. Tree bark was even ground for flour.

For years some sons either went farther north to look for available land or into the mountains to look for a space suitable for a house and stable. Sometimes these farms seemed to cling to the very mountain wall and it looked as though family members could fall off their farm. For many, the only opportunity for employment was to work as a servant for other more fortunate families. Times were very hard.

Word of this available land soon reached the Osterdahlen area south of Trondheim. Two families from there traveled north and opened two farms south of the present town of Setermoen. It was in the year 1791 that Eggen and Elvevold were opened, soon followed by others. By 1801 there were 47 people living in the valley.

New arrivals cleared a place to build their home and a barn. If fortunate, they had a cow or two, and a few sheep. They also had a small field, but the government still claimed timber, which covered the mountainsides. In these early years the government feared that if farming failed, the settlers would turn to timber for their livelihood. The government wanted these profits. Today little of the timber here is government owned.

In 1821 two families arrived to claim their land in the north of Bardu Valley. One was Jens Mikkelsen (Jensen) and wife Ingeborg, who opened their farm, Brandmoen. It contained 3,000 acres and today is divided into ten farms. Presently it contains 500 acres, of which 25 are cultivated. Today, four generations later, the farm is still in the family.

Of course, much of it is mountainous. Sheep raising is the farm's principal focus. Each year about 100 ewes are kept over winter. Lambs are born about in May and in March adult sheep are shorn and the wool marketed.

Of the cultivated land, about 25 acres is devoted to growing hay (some clover) for winter sheep food. With winters being seven to eight months long it is necessary to rent other fields to grow enough hay. It is ready to cut and bale around July and stored in sheds.

Around the 8th or 10th of June, grass is beginning to green in the mountains so the mother sheep and their lambs are taken up there to graze. In the early days someone was hired to watch for predatory animals, but today they fend for themselves. Only bucks are kept in a small pasture near the barn.

As sheep are left to roam freely in the mountains there is an ever-present danger of predatory animals. Eagles might take young lambs. Lynx, wolverines and bear are a menace, so when sheep are rounded up in September and brought back to the farm, several are usually missing. In September or October it is time to sell lambs for slaughtering. There is a market for these in the valley. Wool is sold to local factories.

Another settler was Thore Ingebrigtsen (Thoreson) who became owner of the farm, Aasen, with papers issued giving him right to clear the land. The original 2,000 acres has been divided into six farms. In 1996 Aasen had ten acres in hay (clover?) which was harvested by the Brandmoen farmer for his sheep.

Thore was about 20 years old at the time. His first wife died in 1823, leaving no children. In 1825 he married Hannah Olsdatter and they lived at Aasen. By 1845 they had eight children: Ingebregt, Ingeborg, Ole B., Karen, Bersvend, Iver, Jorgine, and Ola A. With five sons, no doubt he was concerned about their future, and was looking to the west in America.

XVII
LAND OF OPPORTUNITY

Word had reached the North of opportunities to be found in America, from those who had already emigrated there. In 1860 Bersvend, Thore's second son, went to America, no doubt to see things for himself . Two men from Malselv, Johan Nilsen from Fleskmo and Iver Andreassen, Fagerli, went with him.

While here in America, Bersvend met Knute Anderson, father of Burnett County, and through him, became interested in the Grantsburg area.

Knute Anderson had come to America from Norway in 1851. After working in lumber camps in Polk County, Wisconsin he came north a day's journey to Burnett County. Here he selected a spot in the woods three miles south of present day Grantsburg. The land was on a tote road, or one traveled by lumbermen to and from the big woods to the north. There he built a large log building which was a place where travelers, especially log haulers and lumberjacks, could spend the night.

Such a place offered rest and safety, good company and substantial food. There were sleeping quarters upstairs, and when overcrowded, beds were made on the floor downstairs.

It was here that Bersvend found out about the big woods, where men could earn real money. He also heard talk of the Homestead Act with its promise of "free" land.

Bersvend wrote to his family on the farm, Aasen, telling of glowing possibilities for a better living. There must have been talk of all the "free" land, for the Homestead Act was passed in 1862. Then the logging industry was booming in Northern Burnett County, offering possibilities for earning badly needed cash.

So impressed were they with Bersvend's report, that his entire family began making plans to emigrate. That is all but Ingebregt, whose wife wasn't interested in going to America. Before long, word had spread throughout Bardu Valley and beyond, telling what Bersvend had written. Many began to think of going to the new land.

On the nearby farm, Brandmoen, Jens Henrik Mikkelsen (Jensen) lived. Jens was married to Ingeborg Ingebrigtsdatter, a sister of Thore Ingebrigtsen from Aasen. They had eight children: Mikal, Trine, Julianne, Ingebrigt, Kari, Kristen, Jens and Marie.

In 1856 Brandmoen had been divided into two parts, one for the older son, Mikal and the other for son Kristen. However, Mikal and Jens decided to join the Thoresons and go to America so Mikal's share went to Kristen. The farm once again was one.

Kristen's son, Kristian took over the farm in 1898. His son Bjarne held it until his son Karstein took over. Today Karstein and his wife, Kristianne live on Brandmoen, the main farm. Karstein is restoring of the old home.

In 1825 Thore Simmons (Thoreson) had claimed the farm, Sundlia, which was near Aasen. He was married to Signe Ingebertson and had four children, a daughter, Bergeth and three sons, Andreas, Tobias and Simon. They, too, decided to go to this new land.

To the north of Bardu lies the commune (township) of Malselv. This was an extension of the river valley and an area with rich soil and great forests. Many years earlier, word of land that was available in North Norway reached the area around Gudbrandsdal, to the south, where conditions were crowded. There Lasses Olson and his son, Ole Lassessen decided to go to this wild and unsettled region long before the Thoresons and Jensens arrived. It is written, "Lassen Olsen and his son Ole Lassessen came here in the summer of 1789. They found a beautiful valley and wild woods and baptized it Fagerlidal," which is what they named the farm they claimed. So wild was the area, Lasse Olsen's second wife perished in the woods about 1801. It was thought that wolves, which had already killed 16 sheep, had attacked her. There were also bears and other wild animals.

Ole had three children. One, born in 1804, was named Tollef Olsen Fagerlidal (Tollefson). He in turn had seven children. One, a son, named Eric Tollefson, was born in 1834.

Fagerlidal lies not far to the north of Bardu on the Malselv River. Also, Eric Tollefson was married to Thore Ingebrigtsen's daughter, Karen Kristina, so it is not surprising that Eric and his wife decided to join the group and go to America.

Two others joined these families. One was Torbin Olson, listed in census records as stepson on Thore Simmon's farm Sundlie, and Simon Estensen from the farm, Bostad. All together there were fourteen families who came from Bardu to the Grantsburg area.

In the census four years after the folks on Aasen and Brandmoen arrived (1825), there were a total of 25 farms in the valley with a population of 187. In 1845, 20 years later, the population had grown to 536 and there were 51 farms. Much of the valley land was taken up. This may have been a factor in the decision to leave Bardu.

On The Way To A New Land

It must have been well into the summer of 1862 when the 14 families sailed for a new land. Different reports say they were 10 or 12 weeks in crossing the Atlantic. One can only imagine how difficult the crossing was. They may have had to carry their own food supplies and even drinking water. In all probability they traveled steerage for it was the mode of travel most immigrants could afford. That meant there was almost no privacy. Bunks were along walls of the big rooms below deck. There must have been cabins for those who could afford them. A story is told that a mother was giving birth at sea, and the family was so relieved when a woman offered her cabin to assure them of privacy. Often, with little or no ventilation, passengers were seasick. Conditions must have been terrible. What must it have been like when there were storms at sea and you could not get out on the deck? How glad they must have been when their ship reached Quebec, the port where many immigrants landed.

In the meantime Bersvend decided to explore another area as a possible home site for the travelers. He went to New Ulm, an area of good farmland that was well settled, thus having advantages over Grantsburg, which was just being opened to settlement. He already had selected a site there but while he was awaiting his people in La Crosse, word of the New Ulm Indian uprising reached him. He decided it would be better for the party to go to Grantsburg. Life might be harder but it would be safer.

From La Crosse the party of over 30 took a boat up the Mississippi and then the St. Croix to St. Croix Falls. The long walk to Grantsburg, carrying their personal belongings, must have intimidated some. All of the families did not come to Grantsburg that first summer. The Tollefson family genealogy records that Sarah was born in St. Croix Falls on August, 18, 1862, and the Estenson and Jens Jensen families came to Grantsburg a year later. A year or two later it was easier to get to Grantsburg. Sever tells of Anton Hanson's family's trip up the rivers in 1864. He tells that Thore Ingebrigtson Thoreson met them at St. Croix Falls, using one of the two teams of horses in Grantsburg. Knute Anderson owned the other team.

Undoubtedly Bersvend took the new arrivals to Knute Anderson's stopping place from where they must have spread out, looking for some of that "free" land. It didn't take long, because few settlers had claimed land in the vicinity at the time. Thore Ingebrigtson Thoreson claimed land east of where the Grantsburg Town Hall now stands. This must have been on the trail from Anderson's stopping place into what was the beginning of Grantsburg. A total of nine of the Bardu group claimed land within a mile and a half of that corner. Simon Estenson made his claim closer to Anderson, just west of where Bethany Church stands today. His was the first deed recorded in the county. The date was January 20, 1866, for the SE quarter of the SW quarter, Section 35 of Township 38, Range 19. Mikal Jensen also stayed close to Anderson, deciding on the 160 acres just north of Anderson's. It was said that these "Nordlanders" were the first tillers of the soil within several days journey from other settlers—a great exaggeration, I am sure—but they were among the very first around Grantsburg.

XVIII
HADSEL ISLAND

I have never visited the Hadseleon Island area. Information has been hard to find, for it is a very small part of the whole of Norway. It is, however, located well above the Arctic Circle, nearly as far north as Bardu and the Coastal Area. I have passed by it when traveling the Hurtigruten or the Coastal Express on my way to Finnsnes. It does not make a stop at the village of Hadsel but it does at nearby Stokmarknes, which is the town where the Hurtigruten had its origin. It was in 1893 when the D/S Vesteraalen made its maiden voyage from Trondheim to Hammerfest.

There may have been some early connection between Bardu and Hadsel, as it is said two men from Hadsel were with Bersvend Thoreson when he first came to Grantsburg. Or the people who had gone to the Lofotens to fish might have met Islanders over the years. It was Peter A. (Skamfer) Anderson, a native of the Hadsel area, who left his mark on early Burnett County history.

He was an agent for the owner of a vessel carrying emigrants to other countries. He tells about it in a letter published in the Grantsburg paper in January 1896. It was in 1861 when he persuaded 65 people from his home territory to come to America. They set sail for the two-month voyage, arriving in Quebec. From there they journeyed to La Crosse. Peter's brother George, who was already in America, met them there. They then traveled up the Mississippi and St. Croix rivers to St. Croix Falls, arriving in November. It appears they stayed there until joined by Anderson, who had gone on with his brother, George, to Knute Anderson's stopping place.

It seems that some of the immigrants who came with him stayed in the St. Croix area, for it says in his letter, "In the spring of 1863 all the immigrants who came with me came up (to Grantsburg) and took homesteads. In the summer they built their houses and prepared for the coming fall and winter."

Other groups came later in 1863 and in 1866, when Anderson's parents and several others came from the Hadsel area. His letter gave about fifteen names of Hadsel people who came here. The Hadsel genealogies are based on those recorded in our library. Unfortunately, there are no accurate records of all who came from Hadsel.

Peter Skamfer Anderson took claim of 160 acres of land at the southeast part of present day Grantsburg. The Homestead Act was passed in 1862 allowing persons to lay claim to 160 acres of land. It was the year following that his Hadsel folks arrived. Unfortunately, there are no accurate records available giving names of individuals. The 1870 census records many of them, but with only *Norway* given as their birthplace those from Hadsel are hard to identify. Strangely, no local descendents kept in touch with their relatives, as have those from the other two areas.

Hadsel Municipality is a part of Vesteraalen, which is a part of the group of islands we think of as Lofotens. The real Lofotens lie to the south of what is known as Vesteraalen. Hadsel is located near the southern part of Vesteraalen on the island of Hadseleon. Different names were given for the location of a few people coming from there, but for simplicity I have labeled all Hadsel.

These islands have a long history dating to the Stone Age and farther, which was when land cultivation began. It is written of Vesteraalen that it is composed of "mighty mountains, jagged peaks, naked moors and forested hills with shores lined with grassy flat land, peat marshes and heather covered moors." The Vesteraalen group is home to 32,000 inhabitants. Some gather in the five boroughs, of which Hadsel is one, while others live along roads on farms and in residences.

Three of these boroughs (Andoy, Oksnes, and Bo) border the fishing grounds that have made the Lofotens so famous for fishing. Facing the open sea, as the western shores do, they are subject to wild western gales and fierce storms that took many lives of early Lofoten fishermen. Less danger exists today, with countless electronic warning systems. They do have the Gulf Stream warming effect and in some places experience little frost. This makes for a longer growing season. Being at about the same latitude, the sunlight cycle is almost as long as that experienced in Bardu and Senya Island. On the leeward side, often facing a fjord, there are calmer waters and a greater concentration of population, as well as more trade and industry.

These islands have a long history of being easily available to seamen who ventured this far north. As people settled along the shores, farming became important as far back as the Iron Age, or in 500-600 A.D.

A site of that time has been examined and provides a description of a typical farm as follows:

The house served as a shelter for both people and livestock. Some fields were close to the farmyard or were scattered nearby. Barley, being a hardy grain type, was grown, and used to produce food. Livestock and the barley were processed on the farm.

On the beach there were a number of boat sheds. They went out fishing in light craft perhaps 12 to 13 meters long. There were larger sheds for the ships that went on war raids or trading goods, for this is Viking territory.

Iron ore and iron items were likely brought here from the outside world but bog iron was found locally. It was utilized for tools and weapons. This improved the early Nordlanders' standard of living.

By the Middle Ages most land suitable for agriculture was being used, with farms in some places being close together. Then in 1349 Black Death struck the area, which brought great loss of life all over Europe. Soon 70 to 80 percent of the farms were unoccupied, but the best ones were taken over by survivors. It took to the end of the Middle Ages (about 1600) before farms reached the number they were before the Black Death.

It was about this period that Christianity replaced the Norse gods, and churches became a meaningful power in society. This brought Viking people into the common European cultural community.

Changes came about. Taxes were introduced, paid to the king or the church. Fish could be sold or exchanged for grain and other necessities. The king and church put a stop to the local chiefs doing their raids. Traders arrived from the south, bringing grains and other commodities for sale, and returning with fish.

After the 1850s times were more prosperous. Many codfish were caught as they came for annual spawning. Then shoals of herring visited the area, providing fabulous catches. These brought capital to the area, providing funds for developing the region, particularly during the last decade of the 19th century.

Undoubtedly the Hadsel area profited during the mid-January to April surge of fishermen from the north and south. The area now has an influx of tourists, a new source of revenue. Formerly fishermen's shanties lined the shores of fishing stations. Today many have been restored, along with those of recent vintage, to accommodate vast numbers of visitors. Many have been built on stilts and painted red, just as the old ones were.

In early days boats were the main means of connecting these islands with the outside world, as well as with each other. Though boats and ferries are still the means of carrying goods and passengers between some islands, they have good roads. Bridges and tunnels connect some islands as well as the mainland. There is also a busy little airport at Hadsel.

If one were to visit these islands today I am sure you would find many things of interest. There are many museums and culture parks, for they have taken great interest in preserving their past. I read that this "is a fairy tale land spread across a multitude of islands in the high north, untamed, exuberant country, quite awesome in its beauty." At the very heart of it lies the Hadsel area.

XIX
SAGAS AND FOLKTALES

Many stories or sagas have been handed down from Viking times. Vikings were great sailors who discovered Iceland, Greenland and Vinland (or North America). They were also great shipbuilders. Their many stories were preserved as oral traditions but it wasn't until the 1200's that they were written down.

These old Norsemen believed in gods who had great powers and could help people. They also believed there were evil beings who were at war with the gods and brought all the ills to the world. Many stories of these struggles are the sagas that have been handed down to the present.

It is said, "Norway has as many folktales as there are trees in Rogaland." Many a Viking tale that has been handed down no doubt has been embellished over the generations of telling.

Gruesome trolls are critters about whom many a tale has been told. They spent their time making life miserable for some human beings as well as for the gnomes. Trolls belong not only to Norwegians but also to all the Scandinavian countries. They weren't the sharpest of critters however, for they often met more clever creatures.

One tale we all likely heard as children is "Three Billy Goats Gruff" where the two smaller Billy Goats outwitted the troll that lived under the bridge. They convinced him he would have a much better meal if he'd wait for the much bigger Great Big Billy Goat Gruff to pass. When Great Big Billy Goat Gruff saw the other two had made it safely across, he started over the bridge. He challenged the troll to come up and look at his horns, which the critter did, only to be knocked in the water to drown. With the end of the troll, the three goats were free to cross the bridge whenever they wanted to.

Then there were the nisse or barn elves that were thought to be good to have around the farm. There was a time when people believed these supernatural creatures were abroad at Christmas time. Even today some people follow the custom of putting out a special treat for the nisse. If he was forgotten, it was believed the barn brownie might take revenge. If a farm animal died, grain was poor, or there was a fire, nisse were blamed. They were taking no chances.

XX
SPIRIT STORIES

Many of these Norwegian "spirit stories" have been handed down. Here are a few that came from the Sildvik area, which Reidar collected.

A Message

In 1908 or 1909, a small sailboat with three men in it was out in a snowstorm when a steamer collided with it. They were on their way home from the Lofotens. An Edvard Olson rescued the sailboat and its wares, about 2.5 kilometers from Sildvik but the men weren't found.

Mr. Olson had a little girl four or five years old named Annie and early one Sunday morning, when everyone was sleeping, she stood on her bed in the kitchen loft and looked out. She saw three white men coming up from the sea toward the house. She ran to her parents, woke them and said, "You must get up. We are having visitors. There are three white men coming from the sea." The father stood up and looked out but saw nobody. He scolded the girl and said she was only fooling and told her to go back to bed. A few weeks later, the father found some pretty stones near the boat and hid them in the boathouse. A few days later Annie was playing there and heard a loud noise behind her. When she turned around and looked, both the boathouse doors were wide open and there in the doorway stood a big man, dressed in white, looking at her. Then she heard a voice saying, "You must go away from here little girl. You must not be here any longer." And so the door went shut and it became quiet.

How Annie came away from the sea, she does not know. When she told me this story that I have heard from others many times before, she remembered only that she met a woman who came from the spring with water carried in pails on a yoke over her shoulders. Annie was so scared she hid herself in the skirt of the woman and cried. When they had gotten out of her what she experienced, they understood that the three men who had drowned wanted the things that had been saved sent to their families. A message was sent to the families of the men and the people came and got the things. Since then nobody has seen or heard ghosts in the area.

(This is true because I have heard this story from Annie's mouth and it has been known and repeated all these years. Annie died of heart failure two years ago (about 1977.) R.T.

The Silver Watch

At the time this story happened, there were only two farms in Otervika. Better neighbors than Ol' Persa and Per Hansa you must search far to find. If one of them slaughtered a cow or got more fish than was needed, in a blink of an eye there was a meal of fresh food sent over to the neighbor with a greeting. No other form of dividing fence was there, except a big creek or a bridge you could drive over that they owned together. Up in the woods on the hill overlooking the house stood a big roomy barn that had fallen down. By the sea there were two long boat sheds, one on each side of the creek. In each shed there was a long tar painted boat that waited to be put in the ocean.

During Christmas when beer should be tasted, ever so often the women would go in one of the boathouses and take their husbands home. The two men had sat drinking and talking about the year's fishing outlook so long they had developed "ocean going sea legs" so the women chased them home and got them in their own beds.

In the winter of 1873, they went to Ballstad in the Lofotens to fish as they had always done and as usual both men lived in the same fishing cabin.

One day in March while they were fishing in Vestfjorden, Per Hansa heard a terrible roar in the west. When he stood up and saw the black cloud coming toward them, he was scared stiff. "Hurry up, men, we are getting bad weather," he called to the nearest boats, but he had barely said the last words when the storm came over them with full force. Anxious hands with sharp knives cut the nets free. A little sail was hoisted and then began a wild sailing, which for many of them would be their last trip toward land. That day Per Hansa had been catching many fish, so he was one of the last to leave. He started off and concentrated on sailing. As long as the air was clear everything went fine, but when big wet snowflakes began to fall, it was more difficult to sail.

What had happened, or where or how, Per Hansa never found out but when land was closer, they heard a cry from the water. When the snow let up a little they saw Ol' Persa and his son sitting straddled over the boat out at the margin of the sea. Per Hansa wanted to go out to rescue them but his men refused to go and told him to take care of himself. Per Hansa had to give up.

Along came five men who were soaked to the skin and frozen. They were men from the ship, Havsula, (Ol' Persa's boat), and they had been rescued. Per Hansa stood in the middle of the floor and pleaded with them to help. He went over to the 17 year old boy who was the son of Ol' Persa. He grabbed him by the collar and yelled at him, "What have you done with your father, boy?" The boy answered, "He didn't want to go with us to land."

Then Per Hansa went over to a corner, turned to the wall, drew a blanket over his head and there he lay until the next day. By then the weather was better and he woke the men and went searching. The Havsula boat was found unharmed and Per Hansa stayed on land for three days and helped Erick (Ol' Persa's son's name), who had now become the head man, ready the boat for sailing. That winter Per Hansa took many trips along the coast with and without a boat. Everyone knew what he was looking for.

The Lofoten fishing was over and there was an easterly breeze. The boats were heading homeward in Vestfjorden. Per Hansa sat and hummed to himself, which he often did when in good humor. The length of the boat and a little to the left came the boat, Havsula with full sail, with the sea in foamy waves along the bow and sides. When he was aware of the boat coming, Per Hansa turned his head to look for Erick. His glance froze, but then he bent forward and to his friends whispered half out loud, *"He is dead—free from pain—not freezing, the old man."* Both the friends saw that Ol' Persa sat there with a wool shirt on, wrong side out, and was picking the lice from it.

Spring, summer and fall went without anyone knowing anything about Ol' Persa. But when Christmas Eve came, and Per Hansa came to the storehouse to get some beer, Ol' Persa sat on the doorstep and blocked the way of Per Hansa who stood for a long time and stared at his neighbor. Then he gathered himself together and said, "Ol' Persa, you know as well as I do that I wanted to rescue you that day at Lofoten. My men forbade me to go out and said they would take the pilot's wheel from my hands if I tried anything like that. But come to me the first night we sleep at Lofoten and tell me where you are laying. Then I will get your body if I have to carry you to the cemetery in a sack. That I promise you, Ol' Persa." When Per Hansa said this, Ol' Persa broke away and disappeared in the smoke.

The first night he slept at Lofoten, Ol' Persa came to Hansa in a dream and carefully told him where he lay. So well did he tell it that Per Hansa and the boatmen had no trouble finding the place. In the stone cliff they found the skeleton wedged in the rocks, Per Hansa had to break it in pieces, put it in a sack and carry it back to the boat. As they were walking away, Per Hansa saw something shiny down in the sand. He bent down and picked up a silver watch. With shaking fingers, he opened the cover, but when he saw that "OP" was engraved in it, he was sure it was Ol' Persa's earthly possession they had found.

He bought a few board ends, nailed them together for a casket that he placed the bones in. When he came home he had a regular funeral for his friend and neighbor. Since then no one has seen or heard of Ol' Persa.

XXI
EARLY EDUCATION IN BARDU

Kristianne Brandmo, who has taught public school in Bardu Valley, wrote these items on education. E.K.

Education has always been given high priority in Norway. Norwegians were fairly literate at an early period. The first people who came to Bardu in 1791 had to be teachers of their own children. They had been learning to read, write, and work math problems along with Lutheran religious instructions. Here there were no school buildings.

The first people here wanted a church but were not allowed to build one until 1821, which was finished in 1829. (Still used today.) They needed someone to help the pastor (klokker) so a young man came who could also work as a teacher.

He had to go from home to home, (likely to the biggest house in the area). A long table and two long benches were hauled from place to place along with him and the books. Some children lived a long way from the "school" house. They had to sleep there so brought their food and bedding with them. The food was brought in pails and consisted of milk, butter, some potatoes, flat bread, boiled meat from calves or lambs, and meal to be boiled into porridge. There were no fish in Bardu unless caught in streams or lakes.

Each child had six weeks of school but later it became 8 to 12 weeks. They were expected to learn to read at home before seven years old, but sometimes that wasn't possible. People of the house where school was held had the meals to prepare and their own work to do. Sometimes they assisted the teacher and at times even disturbed the routine.

Children were expected to attend school from ages 7 to 14 or 8 to 15. Often the smallest cried when the parents dropped them off. However, many were glad, for it gave them other children to talk to and to play with, and they didn't have to be working at home. The teacher often stayed for a two week period at a given home, then moved on to another. Families had to pay the teacher and for the books.

From 1842 there were two teachers in Bardu and in 1882 they had their first school building. By 1896 they had school buildings in ten places. Later there were four more. Farmers gave timber and helped build the buildings. Later they received money from Troms Fylke.

By 1930 the youngest had 16 weeks in school each year and the oldest had 18 weeks. Later they had two weeks of "practical" education (sewing and knitting for girls; woodworking for boys). Now all are together.

Bardu Education In World War II

The airport at Bardufoss was built in 1937 and it was in 1940 that Germans moved into the valley to take over the airport. Kristianne Brandmo tells of the effect on those living there.

When the Germans moved in, schools were closed April 14 and couldn't open until September. This wasn't true at all places in the valley but it was at Bardu because we are near the airport. There were Norwegians who turned Nazi, siding with the German Nazis and in 1942, they and the Germans tried to force the teachers to join them. All the teachers in Bardu refused so schools here were closed from the 17th of March to the 18th of May. I wasn't happy for I liked school.

In September 1944 Germans moved in from the north and took over every house they could find as well as the schoolhouse for quarters so there was no school at all.

In Finnmark, the county north of Troms County, it was much worse. Some children received only four or five years of education during the seven years. In 1944 the Germans burned most homes and sent the people to southern Norway. Those people had the worst time of all Norway during the war.

XXII
WILD ANIMAL LIFE

With many mountains which are sparsely populated, it is little wonder wild animals flourish. Nature is in control. Among animals in the north there are bear, lynx, wolverine, fox, elg (moose to us), a few wolves, lemming and others besides the sea eagle. Many of these are not friendly to a farmer with domestic animals.

One of the most interesting of those named is the lemming. It is a mouse–like rodent seldom seen by anyone. It is small, with yellow and black or gray hair. It seldom leaves its nest except at night when it feeds on local vegetation. One interesting thing is the rate at which it multiplies. An average litter is as many as 10 young. When an average female bears as many as three or four litters a year, it is little wonder the total population is soon overcrowded. It is then the lemming migrates. By the millions, they eat their way, always heading toward the ocean. They are one huge pack, so when they come to a seaside cliff there is no stopping. There are so many in the rear, their weight pushes most of them into the ocean. Only those in the very rear survive to go back and repeat the cycle. It's a strange way for nature to maintain a balance.

Scientists no longer believe that lemmings have suicidal tendencies. Lemmings periodically do migrate from their area when population strains the food supply. Then they swim across streams, rivers, even lakes in order to find food. Sometimes they try to swim bodies of water too long or too deep and so drown in great numbers. Undoubtedly this is what gave rise to the story of mass suicide.

The fox is another animal found here. More important are the fox raised on fur farms. On the island of Dyroy, which lies not far south of Sorreisa, fur farming has long been a tradition, and in 1933 a strange event occurred. An unusual fox cub was born in a litter of silver fox. Fortunately, it was not destroyed. Instead it was kept to sire a breeding stock known as the "Platinum Fox." So rare and beautiful they were, that the first platinum fox furs were given to the Queen of Norway and Eleanor Roosevelt.

Then there is the moose (there it is called elg). It is very much like our moose and a favorite for hunters. There is a hunting season well into September. In the fall of 1996, I saw a helicopter flying by and beneath it hung a moose hunter's shack. It likely was six or eight feet square and was being carried up on the mountainside for hunting season. No doubt it was the easiest way of getting it up on the wooded mountainside.

I understand bears, wolverines, and lynx are the greatest enemies of sheep farmers who pasture sheep in the mountain in summer. The farmer we visited in Bardu Valley pastured his sheep in nearby mountains from June to September and when it came time to bring them back down, ewes and lambs were missing, likely the victims of these animals.

The long seven- to eight-month winters and accompanying lower temperatures must have their rewards, for I understand there are no snakes in the area. They do have some flies and gnats (like mosquitoes). The lizard, only reptile surviving this far north, is one of a kind. Normally they lay their eggs to be hatched later, which they do in the south, but here the eggs hatch within the female and she bears the young alive.

XXIII
BEAR STORIES

The bear has long been an enemy of sheep in North Norway and many stories are told from earlier days. Several follow. These bear stories came from the Bardu Roots Festival book published in 1987. Kjell Hovde put the book together.

BJORNE (bear) ERIC

Erik Simonsenn Stromser and his wife Kirsti Larsdatter Fasetbruen received permission to clear a large area of wilderness in 1839. The possibility of farming there was slim but their intent was to use it as a base for hunting and trapping wild animals found in the valley and mountains. The buildings at Stromsor today were probably built around 1840-1900. There is a house, storehouse, barn with hayloft, and smithy. Earlier there was also a summer barn, grain barn and a well.

Erik Simonsen was a well-known bear hunter and there are many stories of his adventures.

Often Lapps asked Erik to help them with bear plagues. Once he and his son-in-law, Anders Dahlberg, shot three bears near Vetlvatnet. The mother was so large its head dragged along the ground as it was carried on a long sled. In many dramatic situations Erik didn't have time to reload his gun. In such cases, he had to defend himself with a knife or spear.

One summer they had four cows, three of their own and one that was rented. A bear came and killed the three but spared the rented one. It was a hard experience to bear. Such a turn of events could be enough to bankrupt some farmers. Kristi cried but Erik took revenge. It was not an idle boast that he was called Bjorne Erik. It was his life's work.

One time while on the way home from a fishing trip at Altevatnet, Erik set his eye on three bears lounging on a mountain ledge. He loaded both guns and took his daughter, Berit, along to carry the smaller one. They stealthily crept up to the ledge. Erik took aim at the largest bear and in a blink of an eye, down rolled the mother bear. Then Berit quickly handed Erik the second gun. He shot and down came the second, rolling into the lap of the first one.

Casting Lots

One summer day Lars Eriksen Sorgard was working in his seter in Sordalen. As he stopped to take a break and stretch, he noticed a bear in a field across the river from his farm. In those days it was seldom a man went out in the woods without his gun. Lars gingerly crept toward the bear, aimed and shot. The animal was wounded but managed to run up in the mountain. In hot pursuit, Lars followed a clear trail of blood to the bear's lair.

There was no point in waiting for the bear to come out. He went back down to the village, routed out his two brothers and started back up the mountain, intending to smoke the bear out of his cave. They managed to make a pretty good smoke blanket but still no bear came out. Two hours passed. As they began to tire from emotional strain, they joked about going into the lair. Ole Eriksa, the youngest, suggested they cast lots, but to his chagrin, it fell to him. "Yes, well, he needed to go home and milk the cows first," but the others wouldn't hear of it. As he crept into the hole the other two made sick jokes about his being eaten. He made the remark that it was unlikely he would be delivered as was the prophet Jonah. As the dark and smoky cave widened, he heard a growl coming from somewhere quite near. He pushed the gun barrel around the corner of the rock wall. It hit rock. He moved it up and touched something soft. At that moment, the bear slapped the gun so hard with his paw that Ole almost dropped it. Through the retching smoke, he saw two green pricks with something white under them. The bear bared his teeth and Ole shot. The bear fell from the rock waving his paws furiously. The frantic activity created such a stir that Ole sensed there was wind. With a gasp Ole cried, "Help me. I'm suffocating!"

When they came out into the daylight, one could have mistaken Ole for a black bear, so dark was his skin.

Smart Bear

The first farmers at Rydningen Nedre, in particular the son of Jon Simonsen, had many stories of encounters with bears while shepherding. One time Iver Jonssonner and Simon came across a bear that lay under a very steep cliff. It was dining leisurely on a sheep. Iver wanted to climb down and kill the monster, but Jon, who was older, advised him against the deed.

Later they put out bait with a gun triggered so that when the bait was touched the gun would go off. The crafty old bear was smarter than they thought; It tore up chunks of moss, cast it at the trap. The gun fired and the bear went off with the meat. Iver tried again to avenge his sheep, but to no avail. The old beast was too crafty. Jon did manage, as a boy, to kill a bear that had climbed up a birch tree.

Another time the five brothers, Simon, Iver, Martin, Johan and Ole Rydningen were hunting. They combed the woods and found the bear they were looking for. Simon shot but didn't succeed in killing it. The great beast raised itself on its hind legs, battered its front paws and was about to strike Simon. Luckily, Iver also had his gun ready, shot the bear and killed it. The bear was so huge, it took the five brothers a great deal of puffing and straining to drag it into the community. There was a feast that night, as the valley folk came to congratulate the boys for killing the pesky beast. This happened in 1878.

At Rydningen farm there were two splendid dogs, Karo and Peik. Both were unusually sharp and could detect a bear from a very long distance. They worked as a team. Peik, who was long legged and fast, sniffed out the bear trail while Karo kept watch over the sheep. Peik's barking and whining worried the bears and at the same time informed Karo to come join in the sport. They ran many miles through the woods, over the mountains, after the bears. Late at night the dogs would come home, worn out but proud of a good day's work. The bears were so frustrated that summer, they hardly dared to come around the livestock.

Bears did a lot of damage between Rydningen and Strand in those days. Once a man from Sorreisa, Jo Plassa, came to Strand and slept there over night. He left his horse with the Strand horses but shackled it. In the night it was struck down and mutilated.

The Suitor and the Bear Tracks
Early one April morning, about 110 years ago, there was a man who was courting in Nedre Bardu. He was both very tired and nearsighted. New snow had fallen during the night, and on his way he discovered fresh tracks crossing his own. He did not think it could be anything but a bear, awakened from its long winter's nap, out for a bit of fresh air in the woods. Strangely enough it walked only on its back feet. Quickly he informed people of the alarming news, which was received with delight by a number of sharpshooters. In no time they were on their way. It was quite a distance but eventually, with tense excitement, they saw movement in the bushes near where the tracks had been spotted by the suitor. Before shooting they thought it best to get a good look at the bear through the gun viewfinder. After all it was a dangerous maneuver to kill a bear. Suddenly the bear rose from a squatting position behind the bushes and continued forward through the snow. It was discovered that the "bear" was a man out on a lawful errand in the woods, who had soft soled moccasins on his feet. The man hoisted up his pants and secured them around his waist before continuing further, without realizing that there were several gun barrels ready to burn a hole through his back. Both the hunters and suitor received many poignant comments about the incident once the story was known.

XXIV
NORTH NORWAY TODAY

Norwegians have three national hobbies or recreational activities that they likely participate in. Included are angling, skiing and berry picking, which are wonderful family activities, things that all members can join in. They provide exercise as well as giving the family a feeling of togetherness.

Berries can be found in late summer where they grow in swamps or on mountains, easily reached by most families. Blueberries, raspberries, lingonberries, and cloudberries, are found, all of which are delicious as sauce or jams.

There is always fishing, be it in ocean waters, in fjords or in interior streams or lakes. Fish are an important part of the diet because they are easily available. The prize of several kinds of fish is salmon, found in many streams.

Hunting is another activity in which many local people take part. Many tourists come from other countries to enjoy hunting and salmon fishing. There are many different animals to hunt. Included are wolf, bear, wolverine, lynx and of course elg, or as we call it, moose. Many of these are a menace to sheep, which are sometimes left in the mountains for summer pasture. Another hardy sport some people seem to enjoy is ice or glacier climbing. There are glaciers available the year around.

Hiking is another activity many Norwegians and tourists enjoy. One seldom sees a fence and there are many trails through mountains that are well marked, and with cabins at convenient distances. Users are expected to leave them as they find them.

Tourists are encouraged to take part in most of these activities. A bicycle can be rented for trail riding as can rafts and boats for water activities. You can go bird watching, as many different birds nest here. During migration, thousands fly through here on their way to and from the European mainland. There are hundreds of gulls, kittiwakes and puffins, some of which nest in the cliffs. There are sea eagles and eiderdown ducks, the latter having been a moneymaker for local people. The mother duck lines her nest with down of her feathers. Nests were "robbed" of down because it is great for wadding pillows and quilts as well as filling for winter jackets.

There are many museums to visit. They are about art, birds, boats, history, the Northern Lights Planetarium, and countless other things. There is always the Hurtigruten (Norwegian Coastal Voyage) where you can take the "world's most beautiful voyage" while relaxing and enjoying the scenery.

Fishing Today and the Economy

Malselv's river mouth is not far from Bardu Valley. Being subject to tides, it is gateway to one of the Atlantic salmon spawning grounds. Salmon enter the river here, which flows through fairly level land until it reaches the Malselvfossen, a waterfall, which has been harnessed for electrical power. Before dams were built, salmon could get over the natural falls without difficulty. So that salmon may reach their breeding grounds upriver, fish ladders have been built in today's falls. Beneath the falls lies a pool with its wealth of salmon. The government sells rights to fish from the pool. Because the price is very high, a limited number enjoy the privilege. The government controls all salmon fishing rights, which is an important source of revenue. The Malselv has a reputation of being the world's leading Salmon River.

Fishing has always been and still is an important part of Troms County's economy, but the coastal area has seen great changes. No longer are most men taking a January to April trip to the Lofotens to supplement what their seaside farm produces. Today industries have sprung up along the coast, offering employment within commuting distance. Very few working farms with red barns are seen, which once was such an important part of their existence.

Fish still play an important part in Norway's economy. Recent figures show that five percent of Troms" population is involved in fish. However, everything has changed since the 19th century. No longer are they facing cold, blustery weather in open fishing boats. Now there are many fish farms, which offer employment and produce salmon and trout for food, much of it canned or frozen. A few produce cod, char and shellfish.

There are also numerous fish hatcheries producing salmon, trout and char stock. Fish are still an important part of the economy, especially on the islands, but a far cry from Lofoten days.

Another event, which brought drastic changes to the Norwegian economy, was the discovery of oil on the country's continental shelf. Petroleum and gas sales have brought new sources of government revenue, as well as employment for the four million inhabitants. Nearby European countries prove to be a ready market for these products.

Genealogies

The genealogies that follow are of some of the early Grantsburg settlers. There are three groups. Those from (1) the Coastal Area near Sorreisa, (2) Bardu Valley, and (3) Hadseleon Island (Hadsel). The information in these may not be accurate but it is as it was given to Henry Peterson for his genealogy records. For one thing, the birthplace of an individual may not be right. Often it was given as North Norway so various clues have been used to find a more accurate location, or the name of a local neighborhood may have been given, which can't be found on maps. Names of some towns are duplicated and found in more than one place in Norway.

I've limited the genealogies to those who came from these three localities. The coastal area and Bardu are somewhat farther north than Hadsel, which is about at the 68½ north latitude. The other two are closer to the 69th parallel, but they have much in common.

The following key will assist in knowing meanings as you read the genealogies:

b	Place of birth
em	Date of emigration
F	Female
M	Male
2	Second generation child
*	Spouse
m	Date of marriage
N	Norway

Note --Dates of birth and death given thus: 1826-1910.
If born in America, no place of birth is given in these genealogies.

Coastal Area

The Coastal Area or the Senja and Sorreisa genealogies are fewer in number. For this reason I have included not only the ones who emigrated in the 1860s, but also those who came a few years later, most to the Wood Lake area. Not as many from the coast left their homeland, likely because there were more ways to earn a living near the sea. There was always fishing and a market for the fish as well as work related to ocean shipping. In the Bardu area farming was about the only means of livelihood at this period.

Clementson, Adolph Martin – 1851-1939 – b Senja Island, N - em. 1868
  *Thomassen, Theanna – 1843-1913 – b Sorreisa, N
        m 1870 – em 1868
      2 M Clementson, Knute – 1870-1945
                *Erickson, Nernine – m 1898
      2 M Clementson, Andrew –1872-1975
                *Haug, Elsie – m 1905
      2 F Clementson, Mary – 1875-1946
      2 F Clementson, JoHannah – 1877-1958
                *Kanne, Theodore – m 1902
      2 F Clementson, Anna – 1880-1911
                *Tollefson, Emil – m 1901
      2 M Clementson, Arthur – 1882-1960
                *Haug, Anna – m 1908
      2 M Clementson, Franklin – 1885-1958
                *Hale, Kate – m ——
      2 M Clementson, Stanley – 1887-1958
                *Amundson, Ida – m 1916

Torgerson, John – 1855-1932 – b Finland, N – em. 1880
  *Carlson, Olea – b Trondheim N – m 1883
      2 F Torgerson, Tina –1884-1934
                *Haakseth, Olaf – m 1907
      2 M Torgerson, Iver – 1886-1931
                *McCullough, Margaret – m ——
      2 F Torgerson, Mayme – 1888-1976
                *Gortmaker, John – m ——
      2 M Torgerson, John – 1891-1973
                *Wagenius, Ida – m ——
      2 F Torgerson, Ragna – 1893-1965
                *Wagenius, Bennie – m 1914

2 F Torgerson, Hannah – 1895-1987
      *Lien, Ole – m 1916
2 F Torgerson, Sylvia – 1897-1937
      *Thurlow, Frank – m ——
2 M Torgerson, Silas – 1899-1976
      *Trolin, Gladys – m ——-
2 M Torgerson, Herman – 1902-1995
      *Cuthbert, Ruth – m 1925
2 M Torgerson, Herbert – 1903-1905

Thompson, Andrew – 1846-1915 – b Sorreisa, N – em 1871
      *——, Mary – m 1875
      2M Thompson, Albert – 1876-1948
            *Larson, Ida – m 1905
      2F Thompson, Josephine – 1879-1971
            *Nolan, Tom – m 1901
      2M Thompson, Martin – 1881-1962
            *Moan, Amanda – m 1910
      2M Thompson, Arthur – 1884-1979
            *Metzger, Leda – m ——
      *Lund, Helen – m 1889
      2M Thompson, M. William – 1890-1972
            *Hegge, Elvira – m ----
      2M Thompson, Roy – 1893-1916
      2F Lund, Alma – 1884-1960 (child of Helen Lund)

Thompson, Christian – 1836—— – b Sorreisa, N – em 186--
      *Jacobson, Margrete –1831- —— – m ——
      2F Thompson, Anne – 1863——

Hanson, Ellert – 1860-1921 – Senja Island, N – em 1886
      *Balzersdatter, Sofie – m 1892
      2M Hanson, Harold – 1893-1966
            *Johnson, Mamie – m 1931
      2M Hanson, Emil – 1895-1986
            *Nelson, Ella – m 1924
      2M Hanson, Clarence – 1897-1979
            *Nelson, Annie – m 1926
      2M Hanson, Odin – 1899-1981
            *Schuneman, Alice – m 1943
      2F Hanson, Nellie – 1902-1943

Hanson, Ingvard – 1853-1935 – b Senja Island, N – em 1879
   *Balzersdatter, Jensine – m 1877
        2M Hanson, Bernhard – 1878-1893 – b Senja Island
        2M Hanson, Hans – 1880-1893
        2M Hanson, Carl – 1882-1937
                *Biederman, Anna – m 1925
        2F Hanson, Tina – 1884-1893
        2F Hanson, Emilie. .1885-1893
        2F Hanson, Anna . .1887-1970
                *Biederman, Paul – m 1909
        2M Hanson, Emil – 1889-1893
        2M Hanson, John – 1891-1967
                *Hegge, Minnie – m 1921
        2F Hanson, Clara – 1893——-
                *Haugen, Jacob – m 1912
        2F Hanson, Tina – 1895-1989
                *Rasmussen, Ole – m 1936
        2M Hanson, Herman – 1899———
                *Nilsen, Bertha – m ———
        Five children died of diphtheria in Sept. 1893.
        All buried same day.

Martinson, Balzer – 1828-1906 – b Ibestad, N – em 1877
   *Sorensdatter, Maren – ——-1884 – m 1856
        2F Balzersdatter, Jensine – 1854-1947 – b Finland, N
                *Hanson, Ingvard – m 1877
        2F Balzersdatter, Sofie – 1856-1941 – b Senja, Is, N
                *Hanson, Eilert – m 1892
        2M Martinson, Mekal – 1863-1945 – b Finland, N
                *Torvelson, Mathilda – m 1888
   *Olsdatter, Karen – 1822-1914 – m 1887

Martinson, Mekal – 1863-1945 – b Finland, N – em 1887
   *Torvelson, Mathilda – m 1888
        2F Martinson, Joakim (Kima) – 1889-1969
                *Ryss,Albert – m 1915
        2M Martinson, Benjamin – 1893-1947
                *Amundson, Esther – m ———
        2M Martinson, Olaf – 1897-1950
        2M Martinson, Ingbert – 1901-1983
                *Magnuson, Lillian – m 1929

Bardu Area

The Bardu area genealogies have been the easiest to assemble. For those who came in 1862 in Bersvend Thoreson's group, there are quite complete records. Many of their descendents here have kept in contact with the homeland. They were the first large group of immigrants to arrive here in Grantsburg. In the Bardu area farming was about the only means of livelihood at this period. Three families besides Knute Anderson were known to be here near Grantsburg when they arrived. They were the Hickersons, Dotys and Adam Seed. There are excellent records for the Hickersons, including a history of the family, but little on the others.

Ingebretson, Thore (Thoreson) – 1801-1894 – b S Norway – em 1862
  *Olson, Hanna – 1806-1894 – b S Norway – m ——
       2M Thoreson, Swen – —— ——
       2F   Thoreson, Ingeborg – —— ——
           *Higden, A. – m ——
       2M Thoreson, Ole B – 1829-1905 – b Bardu
           *Anderson, Anne – m 1856
       2F   Ingebretson, Karen – 1832-1899 – b Bardu
           *Tollefson, Eric – m 1861
       2M Thoreson, Bersvend, – 1835-1929 – b Bardu
           *Johnson, Mary – m 1895
       2M Thoreson, Iver – 1937-1914 – b Bardu
           *Johansdatter, Olea – m 1873
       2F   Thoreson, Jorgine – 1883-1875 – b Bardu
           *Olson, Oliver – m ——
       2M Thoreson , Ola A. – 1845-1934 – b Bardu
           *Helman, Albertina m. 1876

Thoreson, Ole B – 1829-1905 – b Bardu – em 1862
  *Anderson, Anne – m 1856
       2F   Thoreson, Hannah – 1859-1941 – b Bardu
           *Hegge, Jacob – m 1880
       2M Thoreson, Tollef – 1862-1943 – b Bardu
           *Thoreson, Ingaborg m ——
       2M Thoreson, Henry – 1867-1943 – b Bardu
       2F   Thoreson, Caroline –1870-1947 – b Bardu
           *Olson, Lydian – m 1891 – b Bardu

Thoreson, Bersvend, – 1835-1929 – b Bardu – em 1860
    *Olson, Isabelle – 1831-1887 – m ——-
        2F Thoreson, Hanna 1860-1868 – b Bardu
        2M Thoreson, Oliver – 1862 ——— – b ——
        2F Thoreson, Isabella – 1866-1947
                *Jensen, James H. – m 1889
        2F Thoreson, Anna – 1867-1938
                *Jensen, Sever – m 1896
        2M Thoreson, Theodore – 1869-1931
        2M Thoreson, Peter – 1873-1930
    *Johnson, Mary – m 1895

Thoreson, Iver – 1837-1914 – b Bardu – em 1862
    *Johansdotter, Olea – m 1873
        2F Thoreson, Hannah – 1874-1955
                *Jensen, John – m 1894
        2F Thoreson, Caroline – 1875-1946
                *Unseth, Nordal – m 1899
        2M Thoreson, Thomas – 1877———

Thoreson, Ole A. – 1845-1934 – b Bardu – em 1862
    *Helman, Albertina – m 1876
        2F Thoreson, Ida – ———--——— – b Minn.
        2F Thoreson, Theresa ———--——— – b Minn.
        2M Thoreson, Olaf ———--——— – b Minn.
        2F Thoreson, Hannah ———--——— – b Minn.
        2M Thoreson, Elmer ———--——— – b Minn.

Thoreson, Thor Simmons – 1800-1876 – b Bardu – em 1862
    *Ingebretson, Signe – m ——
        (Three children died in Norway)
        2F Thoreson, Bessie – 1836-1881 – b Bardu
                *Hagen, John – m ——
        2M Thoreson, Andreas – 1841-1877 – b Bardu
        2M Thoreson, Tobias – 1844-1913 – b Bardu
                *Jensen, Ingaborg – m 1980
        2M Thoreson, Simon – 1849-1918 – b Bardu
                *Nygaard, Isabelle – m 1883

Thoreson, Tobias – 1844-1913 – b Bardu – em 1862

    *Jensen, Ingeborg – m 1880

        2F Thoreson, Tina – 1880-1896

        2M Thoreson, James – 1881-1971

        2F Thoreson, Elvina – 1884——

            *Kruger, Max – m ——

        2M Thoreson, Alfred – 1886-1972

            *Amundson, Anna – m 1913

        2F Thoreson, Clara – 1889-1889

        2M Thoreson, Eddie – 1890-1959

            *Amundson, Jennie – m 1917

        2F Thoreson, Clara – 1893-19--

            *Witt, C. – m ——

        2M Thoreson, Thomas – 1896-1896

        2F Thoreson, Thine – 1897——-

        2M Thoreson, Timmy – 1900-1978

            *Hanson, Evelyn – m 1927

        2F Thoreson, Tina – 1901-1903

        2F Thoreson, Minervia – 1902-1991

            *Cozens, Henry – m ——

        2M Thoreson, Norman – 1905--——

Thoreson, Simon – 1849-1918 – b Bardu – em 1862

    *Nygaard, Isabelle – m 1883

        2M Thoreson, Silas – 1885-1949

            *Tollefson, Flossie – m 1915

            (Daughter died at 3 yrs.)

        2M Thoreson, Herman – 1893-1959

Jensen, Jens – 1836-1917 – b Bardu – em 1862

    *Stenerson, Amelia – m 1857

        2M Jensen, Joe – ——

        2F Jensen, Annie – 1862----- b Bardu

            *Andreason, Andrew – m ——

        2F Jensen, Ingeborg – 1864-1925

            *Thoreson, Tobias – m 1880

        2F Jensen, Jensena – 1866-1889

            *Carlson, Robert – m ——

2M Jensen, Theodore – 1868-1956
      *Anderson, Matilda – m 1899
2M Jensen, Amandus – 1871-1917
      *Peterson, Emma – m 1894
2M Jensen, Simon – 1873-1964
      *Johnson, Helen – m 1894
2M Jensen, Wilhelm – 1876-1925
      *Peterson, Elvie – m ———

Jensen, Michael – 1823-1877 – b Bardu – em 1862
  *Hanson, Marie – 1826-1873 – m 1848
      2M Jensen, Jens – ——- ——-
      2M Jensen, Hans (No records of first five, all born
          in Bardu
      2F Jensen, Isabelle
      2F Jensen, Mary. Two oldest died from eating poisonous
          roots, soon after they arrived. Buried in a travel
          chest. (1862)
      2M Jensen, Iver –
      2M Jensen, Hans – 1856-1932 – b Bardu – em 1862
          *Johnson, Hilma – 1910
      2F Jensen, Mary – ————— – b Gtbg.
      2M Jensen, James J. – 1864-1943 b Gtbg.
          *Thoreson, Isabelle – m 1889
      2M Jensen, John – 1867-1901 – b Gtbg.
          *Thoreson, Hannah – 1894-----

Estenson, Simon – 1822-1914 – em 1862 – with Bardu group
  *Anderson, Anna – 1834-1910 – m ———
      2M Estenson, Edward – 1863-1916
          *Paulson, Hilda – m 1895
      2M Estenson, Hanson – 1869-1869
      2F Estenson, Mary – 1869-1928
          *Bruneau, Meaddy – m 1892

Olson, Torben (Torberg) – —— ——— – b Bardu – em 1862
  *Olsdatte, Beret – 1831——— – b ——-
      2F Olson, Karen – 1857-1939 – b Bardu
          *Halverson, Guttom (Tom) – m 1873
      2M Olson, Simon – 1863——
      2M Olson, Ole – 1868——

Tollefson, Eric – 1834-1900 – b Malselv (Bardu Valley) – em 1862
    *Ingebretson, Karen – 1852-1899 – m 1861
        2M Tollefson, Bernt – 1852-1876 – b Bardu
        2F   Tollefson, Sarah – 1862-1906
                *Anderson, Levi – m 1893
        2F   Tollefson, Anna – 1864-1864
        2M Tollefson, Thomas – 1865-1946
                *Palmer, Ada – m 1896
        2M Tollefson, Henry – 1867-1919
                *Sunfors, Christina – m 1891
        2M Tollefson, Emil – 1869-1935
                *Clementson, Anna – m 1901
        2F   Tollefson, Cerina – 1872-1872
        2M Tollefson, John – (Jan.) 1875—— (died young)
        2M Tollefson, John – (Nov.) 1875——

Halverson, Guttom (Tom) – 1853-1935 – b Bardu – em 1862
    *Olson, Karen – m 1873 – b Bardu
        2F   Halverson, Hannah – 1874-1949
                *Saunders, Chas. – m 1908
        2M Halvorson, Theodore – 1875-1945
                *Ferdinand, Josephine – m 1903
        2F   Halverson, Berit – 1879-1923
                *Johnson, Christian – m 1913
        2M Halverson, Peter – 1880-1967
                *Johnson, Anna – m ——-
        2M Halverson, Eddie – 1882-1957
        2M Halverson, Ole – 1884-1964
                *Griffin, Joy – m ——
        2M Halverson, John – 1886-1904
        2M Halverson, Thomas – 1888-1906
        2M Halverson, Frank – 1891-1972
                *————, Hannah – m ——
        2M Halverson, Simon – 1891-1891
        2M Halverson, Robert – 1893-1977
                *Jensen, Hazel – m 1920
        2M Halverson, Herbert – 1895-1899
        2M Halverson, Casper – 1895-1983
                *O'Keefe, Alice – m 1963
        2M Halverson, Simon – 1899-1970
                *————, Vangie – m ——

Hegge, Jacob – 1850-1933 – b Prestegeld, N – em 1868
    *Thoreson, Hannah – 1859-1941 – m 1880 – b Bardu
        2F Hegge, Albertina – 1881-1969
        2F Hegge, Marie – 1884-1979
        2F Hegge, Jennie – 1886-1958
            *Baird, William – m 1907
        2F Hegge, Alice – 1888-1965
            *Ringstad, David – m ——
        2F Hegge, Sarah – 1889-1928
        2F Hegge, Olga – 1890-1978
        2M Hegge, Henry – 1892-1918
        2M Hegge, Clarence – 1893-1969
            *Olson, Ruth – m 1921
        2F Hegge, Mayme – 1896-1981
        2M Hegge, Wallace – 1898-1966
            *Sullivan, Mae – m ——
Olson, Lydian – 1864-1928 – b Bardu – em ——
    *Thoreson, Caroline – m 1891 – b Bardu
        2M Olson, Lawrence – 1891-1954
        2F Olson, Opal – 1892-1915
        2M Olson, Raymond – 1894-1895
        2M Olson, Walter – 1896- ——
        2F Olson, Mildred – 1898-1956
        2F Olson, Fidelhia – 1899- ——
        2M Olson, Lloyd – 1902-1982
            *Templeton, Charlotte – m 1957
        2M Olson, Leonard – 1905-——
        2M Olson, Earl – 1907- ——
        2F Olson, Grace – 1913-1989
            *Nichols, Norman – m 1940

Haakstad, Ingebrigt – 1825-1901 – Bardu – em
    *Jonsdatter, Sigrid – 1813-1898 – m 1852 – b Bardu
        2F Mattisdatter, Olea – 1860-1945
            *Torgerson, Johan – m 1883

Hadsel Area

I have never visited Hadsel and obtaining information on the area has been difficult. One individual from there was Peter (Skamfer) Anderson, who came here as early as Berswin Thoreson and through his influence many came later in 1863 and 1866. In a letter he wrote in the local paper in 1896 he lists names of people who came from Hadsel, which has been a tremendous help in identifying a few of those who came from there in the 1860s.

Peter (Skamfer) Anderson was one of the first settlers to claim land here, though the Hickersons and Adam Seeds and perhaps others were earlier. He settled on the 160 acres that lie southeast of the intersection of today's Highways 70 and 48/87. I've been told his home is still standing on Highway 70 east of the above intersection.

Skamfer was a name used to designate a certain family or relationship in an area in Norway. With so many with the same surname, it helped identify which person was being referred to. I've read the name was taken from a farm or a hamlet.

Anderson, Peter A. (Skamfer) – 1823-1907 – b Hadsel
        Island – em 1861
    *Eliason, Anna – m 1846 – b Hadsel
        2F Anderson, Ellen – 1847-1931 – b Hadsel
           *Hickerson Perry – m 1866
        2M Anderson, Peter – 1849-1864 – b Hadsel
        2F Anderson, Sophia – 1851-1929 – b Hadsel
           *Branstad, Ole – m 1870
        2M Anderson, Andrew – 1855-1933 – b Hadsel
           *Johnson, Ella – m 1876
        2F Anderson, Petra – 1857-1944 – b Trondheim
           *Hovde, Michael – m 1878
        2M Anderson, Lars – 1859——— – b ——N
        2F Anderson, Anne – 1861-1864
        2M Anderson, Peter C. – 1866———
           *Larson, Johanna – ———
        2F Anderson, Anna – 1870-1962
           *Jensen, Helmer – m 1893
    *Christopher, Helen Anderson – m 1878

Isaacson, Isaac – 1826-1916 – b Hadsel – em 1866
    *Iverson, Sirine – m 1851 – b Hadsel
    (No children)

Hagen, Carl August – 1828-1894 – b Hadsel – em 1861
    *Harrison, Nicholina – ——-1861 – Hadsel – m ——
        2F   Hagen, Mary Jertine – 1859-1930
            *Hoff, Peter – m 1879
    *Anderson, Betsy – m ——
    (Knute Anderson's sister)

Christopherson, John – 1840-1931 – b Hadsel – em 1866
    *Anderson, Hanna – m 1865
        2F   Christopherson, Jessie – 1864-1942 – b Hadsel
            *Johnson, Alfred – m 1891
        2M Christopherson, Adolph – 1866-1954
            – b Atlantic Ocean
            *Norine, Mathilda – m 1892
        2F   Christopherson, Annie – 1869-1954
            *Johnson, Samuel – m 1887
        2M Christopherson, John – 1872-1949
            *Forsman, Christina – m 1899
        2F   Christopherson, Sophia – 1874- ——
            *Fitch, F. A. m ——
        2F   Christopherson, Josefine – 1877-1965
            *Yenna, Ernest – m 1932
        2M Christopherson, Martin – 1879-1961
            *Larson, Indiana – m 1916
        2F   Christopherson, Berntina – 1882-1964
            *Mc Allister, Hugh – m ——
        2F   Christopherson, Jemima – 1885-1893

Johnson, Martin Bount – —— —— – b Hadsel – em 1863
    *Hanson, Hanna Olena – m —— b – Hadsel
        2M Johnson, John A. – —— -——
        2M Johnson, Anton – —— ———
        2F   Johnson, Mary – —— - ——
        Lee, Amund – m ——
        2F   Johnson, Anna – —— ——
        Bains,—— – m ——
        2M Johnson, Peter Juel – 1857-1931
        All five apparently born in Norway

Berg, Ole P. – 1823——— – b – Hadsel – em 1863
   *———, Elizabeth – b – Hadsel – m

Anderson, George (Skamfer) – 1833-1909 – b – Hadsel
     – em 1860 (with Bersvend Thoreson)
   *Hanson, Maren J. – m ———
Anderson, Andrew M. (son of Peter Skamfer) – 1855-1933
     – b Hadsel – em 1863
   *Johnson, Ella – m 1876
          2M Anderson, Alfred P. – 1879-1902
          2M Anderson, Melvin – 1881-1883
          2F Anderson, Melvina – 1883-1908
          2F Anderson, Agnes – 1886-1962
              *Larson, David – m 1914
          2F Anderson, Elfie L. – 1889-1890
          2F Anderson, Elfie May – 1891-1978
          2F Anderson, Olive – 1894-1980
              *Johnson, Henry – m ———
          2F Anderson, Amber – 1896-1967
          2M Anderson, Wallace – 1898-1900

Branstad, Ole Christian – 1839-1906 – b – Moss N – em ———
   *Anderson, Sophie – m 1870 – b Hadsel – (daughter
           of Peter Skamfer Anderson)
          2M Branstad, Peter – 1869-1882
          2M Branstad, Knute – 1872-1873
          2M Branstad, Newton – 1875-1957
              *Paulson, Marie – m 1906
          2F Branstad, Anna – 1879-1879
          2F Branstad, Lillie – 1880-1930
              *Skoglund, John – m 1907
          2F Branstad, Estelle – 1883-1949
              *Norton, Howard – m 1919
          2M Branstad, William – 1886-1893
          2F Branstad, Edna – 1888-1963
              *Pederson, Eli – m 1911
          2M Branstad, Benjamin – 1890-1970
              *Powell, Agnes – m 1952
          2F Branstad, Rhoda – 1893-1979
              *Tyler, Ephraim III – m 1917

Gudmanson, Peter – 1819-1897 – b Hadsel – em 1866
    *------, Mary – 1816-1890 – m ---- b Hadsel
        2M Gudmanson, Adolph

Hoff, Peter – 1852-1912 – b Holand, N. em ----
    *Hagen, Mary Jentine 1859-1930 – b Hadsel
       – em –1861 – m 1879
        2F Hoff, Annie – 1881-1914
            *Anderson, Gust – m ----
        2F Hoff, Louise –1883-1972
            *Anderson, Carl – m ----
        2F Hoff, Clara – 1885-1907
        2F Hoff, Betsy – 1886-1941
            *Nugen, Clarence – m 1919
        2F Hoff, Nellie – 1888-1961
            *Tingy, Robert – m ----
        2M Hoff, Henry – 1889-1962
            *Hagstrom, Effie – m 1942
        2M Hoff, Morgan – 1892-1969
            *Jensen, Mamie – m 1926
        2M Hoff, Walter – 1893-1979
            *Nelson, Agnes – m 1923
        2M Hoff, John – 1895-1971
            *Johnson, Alvina – m ----
        2F Hoff, Ida – 1900-1946

Pederson, Ole Andreas – 1840-1919 – b Hadsel – em 1862
    *Eliason, Eliza – ------ – m 1868
        2M Pederson, Eddie – 1871-1963
            *Olson, Johannah – m 1900,
        2M Pederson,Peter – 1878-1919
            *Thoreson, Tena – m 1897
        2M Pederson, Olaf – ----
            *Paulson, Ida – m ----
        2M Pederson, Eli – ----
            *Simpson, Ethel
        2F Pederson, Annie – ----
            *Olson, Halvor – m ----
        2F Pederson, Linna – ----
            *Eliason, Eli – m ----

Maps

These first maps are of nine sections of land directly south of the village of Grantsburg, plus section 13, which is east of the village and to the north of Highway 70. It was in these sections that the earliest Grantsburg settlers, most of whom came from the three Nordland areas, took their land claims.

The second set is of the nine Wood River sections directly east of the Grantsburg sections. Hadsel settlers took some claims but the Coastal people, particularly those taking claims around Wood Lake, settled more in the 1870's.

Each claim shows two dates. The first is "date of entry" or when the first legal papers were drawn up, while the second is "date of patent," the original conveyance of land to the individual. The then current president of the United States signed this official paper.

Many forties show dates in the 1850's, which was before the Nordlanders arrived. The names of the owners are unfamiliar and in many cases involve claims to as many as ten or twelve forties, obviously not for farming. Many of these larger claims were close to Wood Lake. Frank Becvar's report of tree stumps six feet across, which they found on their farm near Wood Lake when they arrived in 1910, leads me to think these first owners were looking for the largest timber. Another bit of evidence is Luverne Larson's telling of the 100-foot tall tree that took three men to reach around. This grew in a ravine on their farm when he was a boy, which was likely left behind because it was too difficult to remove.

We can assume that it was easier to get these larger timbers to the mills if they were near water, which was where these larger claims were, near Wood Lake. Logs could be piled up on the ice in winter and with the spring thaw would flow to the mouth of Wood River and thus down stream to the St. Croix, and on to Marine and Stillwater to the sawmills. Later Knute Anderson built a dam on Wood River to control the flow of the logs.

In researching the background of my Grandfather's land I found he was not the first owner but had bought one of the three forties from a Hickerson while the other two he got from the government for back taxes. The original landowner in 1857, according to our map, apparently removed a considerable amount of large logs and then let the land go back to the government for taxes. These examples lead me to believe that these earliest owners were primarily interested in the largest timber.

Names of the early scalpers are forgotten but our early Nordlanders came to these lands and became a part of our history.

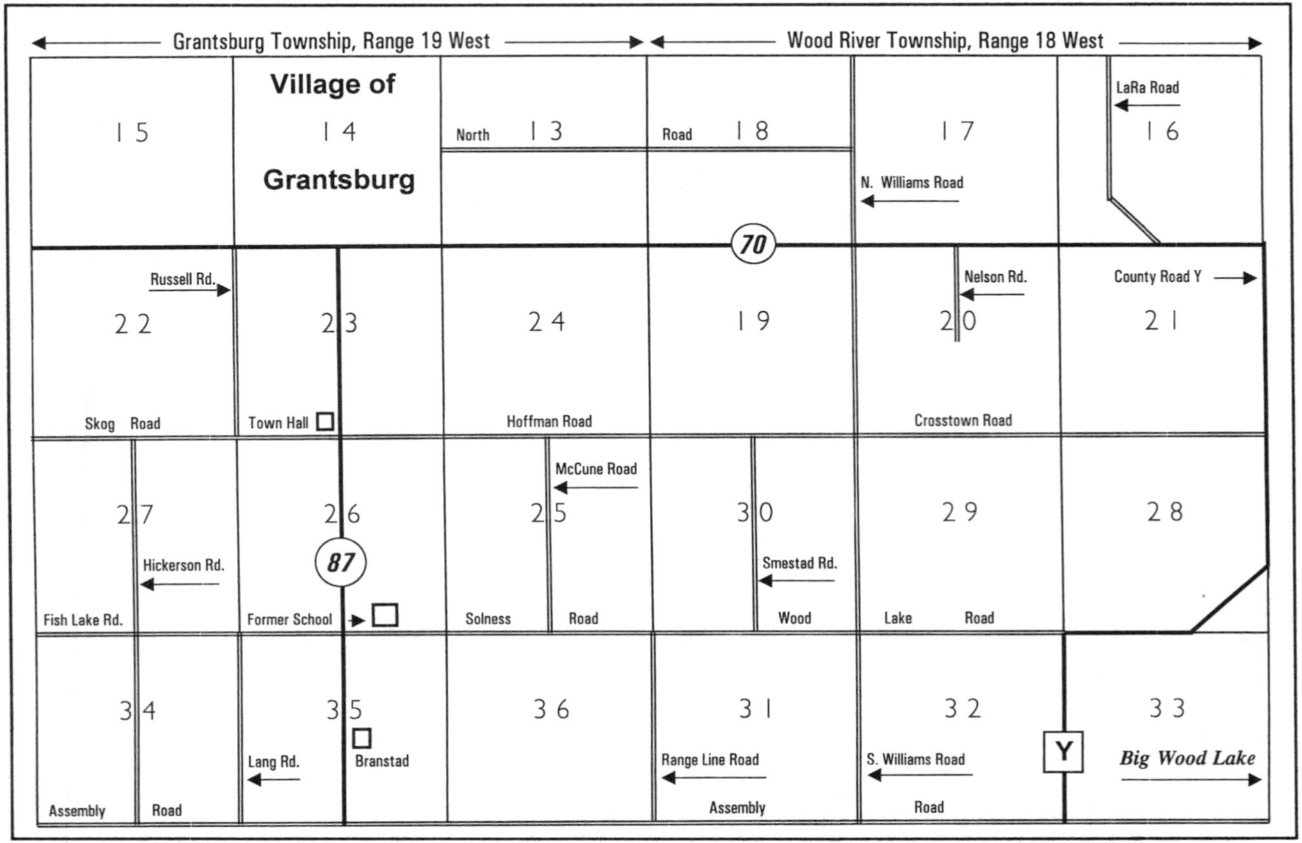
Grantsburg Township, Range 19 West
Wood River Township, Range 18 West
15
Village of
14
Grantsburg
North
13
Road
18
17
LaRa Road
16
N. Williams Road
70
Russell Rd.
22
23
24
19
Nelson Rd.
20
County Road Y
21
Skog Road
Town Hall
Hoffman Road
Crosstown Road
McCune Road
27
26
25
30
29
28
87
Hickerson Rd.
Smestad Rd.
Fish Lake Rd.
Former School
Solness
Road
Wood
Lake
Road
34
35
36
31
32
33
Lang Rd.
Branstad
Range Line Road
S. Williams Road
Y
Big Wood Lake
Assembly
Road
Assembly
Road

Map with numbered squares representing sections in Grantsburg and Wood River Townships.

Key to maps on following pages.

The letters on the maps correspond to the numbered sections as identified below. For example, "G" maps cover Sections 22 and 23 of Grantsburg Township.

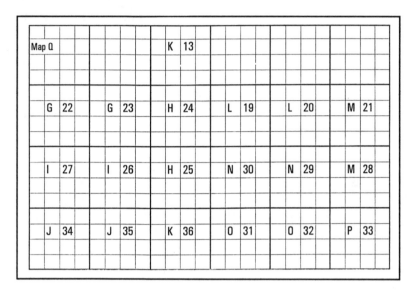

G & H

Section 22, Township 38 N, Range 19 W — Grantsburg Township

JOEL HICKERSON 1869--1871 NW-NW	NOAH UTTER 1888 NE-NW	JOHN PETERSON 1876--1877 NW-NE	SWEN PETERSON 1866--1873 NE-NE
NIMROD HICKERSON 1862--1871 SW-NW	NOAH UTTER 1888 SE-NW	JOHN PETERSON 1876--1877 SW-NE	SWEN PETERSON 1866--1873 SE-NE
NIMROD HICKERSON 1866--1871 NW-SW	NOAH UTTER 1888 NE-SW	PERRY D. HICKERSON 1865--1871 NW-SE	PERRY D. HICKERSON 1865--1871 NE-SE
NIMROD HICKERSON 1866--1871 SW-SW	NIMROD HICKERSON 1866--1871 SE-SW	PERRY D. HICKERSON 1865--1871 SW-SE	PERRY D. HICKERSON 1865--1871 SE-SE

Section 23, Township 38 N, Range 19 W — Grantsburg Township

SWEN PETERSON 1866--1873 NW-NW	ANDREAS OLSEN 1865--1872 NE-NW	PETER A. ANDERSON 1863--1870 NW-NE	PETER A. ANDERSON 1863--1870 NE-NE
SWEN PETERSON 1866--1873 SW-NW	ANDREAS OLSEN 1865--1872 SE-NW	PETER A. ANDERSON 1863--1870 SW-NE	PETER A. ANDERSON 1863--1870 SE-NE
MARTIN B. JOHNSON 1865--1872 NW-SW	ANDREAS OLSEN 1865--1873 NE-SW	Thor Engebright-sen Thoreson 1863--1871 NW-SE	Thor Engebright-sen Thoreson 1863--1871 NE-SE
MARTIN B. JOHNSON 1865--1872 SW-SW	ANDREAS OLSEN 1865--1873 SE-SW	Thor Engebright-sen Thoreson 1863--1871 SW-SE	Thor Engebright-sen Thoreson 1863--1871 SE-SE

Section 24, Township 38 N, Range 19 W — Grantsburg Township

MAGNUS NELSON 1863--1871 NW-NW	MAGNUS NELSON 1863--1871 NE-NW	MARTIN ANDERSON 1865--1872 NW-NE	ISAAC R. ISAACSON 1867--1874 NE-NE
MAGNUS NELSON 1863--1871 SW-NW	MAGNUS NELSON 1863--1871 SE-NW	MARTIN ANDERSON 1865--1872 SW-NE	ISAAC R. ISAACSON 1867--1874 SE-NE
TORBER OLSON 1863--1871 NW-SW	TORBER OLSON 1863--1871 NE-SW	JENS JOHON JENSEN 1866--1872 NW-SE	JENS JOHON JENSEN 1866--1872 NE-SE
TORBER OLSON 1863--1871 SW-SW	TORBER OLSON 1863--1871 SE-SW	JENS JOHON JENSEN 1866--1872 SW-SE	JENS JOHON JENSEN 1866--1872 SE-SE

Section 25, Township 38 N, Range 19 W — Grantsburg Township

BERSVEN THORESON 1876--1876 NW-NW	BERSVEN THORESON 1876--1876 NE-NW	OLE B. THORESON 1865--1872 NW-NE	OLE B. THORESON 1865--1872 NE-NE
ERIC TOLLEFSON 1863--1871 SW-NW	ERIC TOLLEFSON 1863--1871 SE-NW	OLE B. THORESON 1865--1872 SW-NE	OLE B. THORESON 1865--1872 SE-NE
ERIC TOLLEFSON 1863--1871 NW-SW	ERIC TOLLEFSON 1863--1871 NE-SW	E. HAKSTAD 1877--1876 NW-SE	E. HAKSTAD 1877--1876 NE-SE
ANTON HANSON 1865--1875 SW-SW	ANTON HANSON 1865--1875 SE-SW	ANTON HANSON 1865--1875 SW-SE	ANTON HANSON 1865--1875 SE-SE

Section 26, Township 38 N, Range 19 W — Grantsburg Township

NW-NW	NE-NW	NW-NE	NE-NE
AND SKOG 1875-1875	IVER THORESON 1867-1875	IVER THORESON 1867-1875	BERSVEN THORESON 1876-1876

SW-NW	SE-NW	SW-NE	SE-NE
NIMROD HICKERSON 1861-1862	IVER THORESON 1867-1875	IVER THORESON 1867-1875	BERSVEN THORESON 1876-1876

NW-SW	NE-SW	NW-SE	NE-SE
CHAS. AMONDS 1857-1860	CHAS. AMONDS 1857-1860	NELS JUUL 1865-1872	NELS JUUL 1865-1872

SW-SW	SE-SW	SW-SE	SE-SE
CHAS. AMONDS 1857-1860	CHAS. AMONDS 1857-1860	NELS JUUL 1865-1872	NELS JUUL 1865-1872

Section 27, Township 38 N, Range 19 W — Grantsburg Township

NW-NW	NE-NW	NW-NE	NE-NE
TOBIAS THORESON 1904-___	THOR SIMMON THORESON 1863-1870	NIMROD HICKERSON 1861-1862	AND. SKOG 1871-1875

SW-NW	SE-NW	SW-NE	SE-NE
P. J. JOHNSON ___-1906	THOR SIMMON THORESON 1863-1870	THOR SIMMON THORESON 1863-1870	THOR SIMMON THORESON 1863-1870

NW-SW	NE-SW	NW-SE	NE-SE
THOS. TOLLEFSON 1901-___	OLE ANDREAS JOHNSON 1870-1871	OLE P. BERG 1863-1870	OLE P. BERG 1863-1870

SW-SW	SE-SW	SW-SE	SE-SE
AND. JACOBSON 1885-1886	OLE ANDREAS JOHNSON 1870-1871	OLE P. BERG 1863-1870	OLE P. BERG 1863-1870

Section 34, Township 38 N, Range 19 W — Grantsburg Township

NW-NW	NE-NW	NW-NE	NE-NE
EDWARD HANSEN 1875-1875	EDWARD HANSEN 1875-1875	EDWARD HANSEN 1875-1875	ADAM SEED 1859-1860

SW-NW	SE-NW	SW-NE	SE-NE
JACOB JACOBSON 1881-1882	JACOB JACOBSON 1881-1882	EDWARD HANSEN 1875-1875	ADAM SEED 1859-1860

NW-SW	NE-SW	NW-SE	NE-SE
JOHN JACKSON ___-1880	JACOB JACOBSON 1881-1882	NELS HANSON 1875-1875	NELS HANSON 1875-1875

SW-SW	SE-SW	SW-SE	SE-SE
HANS HAUGER ___-1888	JACOB JACOBSON 1881-1882	NELS HANSON 1875-1875	NELS HANSON 1875-1875

Section 35, Township 38 N, Range 19 W — Grantsburg Township

NW-NW	NE-NW	NW-NE	NE-NE
ADAM SEED 1859-1860	PETER GUDMANSON 1867-1873	LEWIS OLSON 1857-1860	LEWIS OLSON 1857-1860

SW-NW	SE-NW	SW-NE	SE-NE
ADAM SEED 1859-1860	PETER GUDMANSON 1867-1873	LEWIS OLSON 1857-1860	LEWIS OLSON 1857-1860

NW-SW	NE-SW	NW-SE	NE-SE
PETER ANDERSON 1857-1860	PETER ANDERSON 1857-1860	MIKEL JENSEN 1863-1870	MIKEL JENSEN 1863-1870

SW-SW	SE-SW	SW-SE	SE-SE
PETER ANDERSON 1857-1860	PETER ANDERSON 1857-1860	MIKEL JENSEN 1863-1870	MIKEL JENSEN 1863-1870

K & L

ZACERIAS ERICKSON 1866--1873 NW-NW	ZACERIAS ERICKSON 1866--1873 NE-NW	CHRISTIAN OLSON 1866--1871 NW-NE	CHRISTIAN OLSON 1866--1871 NE-NE
ZACERIAS ERICKSON 1866--1873 SW-NW	ZACERIAS ERICKSON 1866--1873 SE-NW	CHRISTIAN OLSON 1866--1871 SW-NE	CHRISTIAN OLSON 1866--1871 SE-NE
OLE ANDREW PEDERSON 1868--1874 NW-SW	OLE ANDREW PEDERSON 1868--1874 NE-SW	ERIC HANSON 1867--1874 NW-SE	ERIC HANSON 1867--1874 NE-SE
OLE ANDREW PEDERSON 1868--1874 SW-SW	OLE ANDREW PEDERSON 1868--1874 SE-SW	ERIC HANSON 1867--1874 SW-SE	ERIC HANSON 1867--1874 SE-SE

Section 36, Township 38 N, Range 19 W
Grantsburg Township

AUG. ANDERSON 1876--1877 NW-NW	AUG. ANDERSON 1876--1877 NE-NW	GUSTAF LARSON 1876--1876 NW-NE	GUSTAF LARSON 1876--1876 NE-NE
AUG. ANDERSON 1876--1877 SW-NW	AUG. ANDERSON 1876--1877 SE-NW	GUSTAF LARSON 1876--1876 SW-NE	GUSTAF LARSON 1876--1876 SE-NE
HANS OLAI ANDERSON 1863--1870 NW-SW	HANS OLAI ANDERSON 1863--1870 NE-SW	J. A. Christopherson 1865--1872 NW-SE	J. A. Christopherson 1865--1872 NE-SE
HANS OLAI ANDERSON 1863--1870 SW-SW	HANS OLAI ANDERSON 1863--1870 SE-SW	MARTIN ANDERSON 1865--1872 SW-SE	MARTIN ANDERSON 1865--1872 SE-SE

Section 13, Township 38 N, Range 19 W
Grantsburg Township

ISAAC ISAACSON 1876--1874 NW-NW	Gustav Johan ERICKSON 1876--1877 NE-NW	Gustav Johan ERICKSON 1876--1877 NW-NE	F. G. JARL 1876--1876 NE-NE
ISAAC ISAACSON 1876--1874 SW-NW	Gustav Johan ERICKSON 1876--1877 SE-NW	Gustav Johan ERICKSON 1876--1877 SW-NE	LARS JOHN ANDERSON 1876--1877 SE-NE
PEDER OLSON 1876--1876 NW-SW	PEDER OLSON 1876--1876 NE-SW	JENS J. HIGDON 1875--1876 NW-SE	LARS JOHN ANDERSON 1876--1877 NE-SE
PEDER OLSON 1876--1876 SW-SW	PEDER OLSON 1876--1876 SE-SW	LARS JOHN ANDERSON 1876--1877 SW-SE	LARS JOHN ANDERSON 1876--1877 SE-SE

Section 19, Township 38 N, Range 18 W
Wood River Township

CARL E. JOHNSON --1888 NW-NW	CARL E. JOHNSON --1888 NE-NW	JOHN ERICK FORSMAN 1875--1875 NW-NE	JOHN ERICK FORSMAN 1875--1875 NE-NE
CARL E. JOHNSON --1888 SW-NW	CARL E. JOHNSON --1888 SE-NW	JOHN OLSON 1876--1877 SW-NE	JOHN ERICK FORSMAN 1875--1875 SE-NE
ANDERS G. ANDERSON 1876--1877 NW-SW	ANDERS G. ANDERSON 1876--1877 NE-SW	JOHN OLSON 1876--1877 NW-SE	JOHN OLSON 1876--1877 NE-SE
ANDERS G. ANDERSON 1876--1877 SW-SW	ANDERS G. ANDERSON 1876--1877 SE-SW	JOHN OLSON 1876--1877 SW-SE	R. A. SMITH --1888 SE-SE

Section 20, Township 38 N, Range 18 W
Wood River Township

Section 21, Township 38 N, Range 18 W — Wood River Township

JOHN FORSMAN 1875--1875 (NW-NW)	AUG. FORSMAN 1882--1883 (NE-NW)	SWEN DANIELSON 1875--1876 (NW-NE)	SWEN DANIELSON 1875--1876 (NE-NE)
JOHN FORSMAN 1875--1875 (SW-NW)	JOHN FORSMAN 1875--1875 (SE-NW)	SWEN DANIELSON 1875--1876 (SW-NE)	SWEN DANIELSON 1875--1876 (SE-NE)
SEVER JENSEN 1904-- (NW-SW)	JOHN FORSMAN 1875--1875 (NE-SW)	DANIEL ROBERTSON 1856--1859 (NW-SE)	DANIEL ROBERTSON 1856--1859 (NE-SE)
ROBT. A. SMITH 1893--1892 (SW-SW)	ERIC FORSMAN 1876--1875 (SE-SW)	DANIEL ROBERTSON 1856--1859 (SW-SE)	DANIEL ROBERTSON 1856--1859 (SE-SE)

Section 28, Township 38 N, Range 18 W — Wood River Township

DANIEL HIBBARD 1856--1859 (NW-NW)	DANIEL HIBBARD 1856--1859 (NE-NW)	DANIEL ROBERTSON 1856--1860 (NW-NE)	DANIEL ROBERTSON 1856--1860 (NE-NE)
DANIEL HIBBARD 1856--1859 (SW-NW)	DANIEL HIBBARD 1856--1859 (SE-NW)	MOSES GIBSON 1856--1859 (SW-NE)	MOSES GIBSON 1856--1859 (SE-NE)
DANIEL HIBBARD 1856--1859 (NW-SW)	DANIEL HIBBARD 1856--1859 (NE-SW)	MOSES GIBSON 1856--1859 (NW-SE)	CHAS. GILFILLAN 1854--1854 (NE-SE)
LYDIAN OLSON --1885 (SW-SW)	DANIEL HIBBARD 1856--1859 (SE-SW)	MOSES GIBSON 1856--1859 (SW-SE)	WM. O. MAHONEY 1853--____ (SE-SE)

Section 29, Township 38 N, Range 18 W — Wood River Township

J. J. BUCK ____--1876 (NW-NW)	J. J. BUCK ____--1876 (NE-NW)	SAMUEL G. DIMMOCK 1856--1859 (NW-NE)	SAMUEL G. DIMMOCK 1856--1859 (NE-NE)
J. J. BUCK ____--1876 (SW-NW)	J. J. BUCK ____--1876 (SE-NW)	SAMUEL G. DIMMOCK 1856--1859 (SW-NE)	SAMUEL G. DIMMOCK 1856--1859 (SE-NE)
JOHN OLSON 1875--1875 (NW-SW)	JOHN OLSON 1875--1875 (NE-SW)	SAMUEL G. DIMMOCK 1856--1859 (NW-SE)	SAMUEL G. DIMMOCK 1856--1859 (NE-SE)
JOHN OLSON 1875--1875 (SW-SW)	JOHN OLSON 1875--1875 (SE-SW)	SAMUEL G. DIMMOCK 1856--1859 (SW-SE)	SAMUEL G. DIMMOCK 1856--1859 (SE-SE)

Section 30, Township 38 N, Range 18 W — Wood River Township

OLE HANSON 1863--1871 (NW-NW)	OLE HANSON 1863--1871 (NE-NW)	EGBERT JOHNSON 1875--1875 (NW-NE)	EGBERT JOHNSON 1875--1875 (NE-NE)
OLE HANSON 1863--1871 (SW-NW)	OLE HANSON 1863--1871 (SE-NW)	EGBERT JOHNSON 1875--1875 (SW-NE)	EGBERT JOHNSON 1875--1875 (SE-NE)
ANDERS LARSON 1877--1878 (NW-SW)	ANDERS LARSON 1877--1878 (NE-SW)	JOHNSON ENGBRIGTSON 1875--1875 (NW-SE)	JOHNSON ENGBRIGTSON 1875--1875 (NE-SE)
ANDERS LARSON 1877--1878 (SW-SW)	ANDERS LARSON 1877--1878 (SE-SW)	JOHNSON ENGBRIGTSON 1875--1875 (SW-SE)	MARTIN OLSON 1875--1875 (SE-SE)

O & P

ANDREAS OLSON 1867-1874 (NW-NW)	ANDREAS OLSON 1867-1874 (NE-NW)	MARTIN OLSON 1875-1875 (NW-NE)	MARTIN OLSON 1875-1875 (NE-NE)
ANDREAS OLSON 1867-1874 (SW-NW)	ANDREAS OLSON 1867-1874 (SE-NW)	MARTIN OLSON 1875-1875 (SW-NE)	JAMES WILLARD 1856-186- (SE-NE)
CHRISTIAN THOMPSON 1876-1876 (NW-SW)	CHRISTIAN THOMPSON 1876-1876 (NE-SW)	ERIC ERICKSON 1876-1876 (NW-SE)	JAMES WILLARD 1856-1860 (NE-SE)
CHRISTIAN THOMPSON 1876-1876 (SW-SW)	CHRISTIAN THOMPSON 1876-1876 (SE-SW)	ERIC ERICKSON 1876-1876 (SW-SE)	JAMES WILLARD 1856-1860 (SE-SE)

Section 31, Township 38 N, Range 18 W
Wood River Township

CALEB COOK 1856-1860 (NW-NW)	CALEB COOK 1856-1860 (NE-NW)	SAMUEL G. DIMMOCK 1856-1860 (NW-NE)	SIMON THORESON ----1883 (NE-NE)
CALEB COOK 1856-1860 (SW-NW)	CALEB COOK 1856-1860 (SE-NW)	SAMUEL G. DIMMOCK 1856-1860 (SW-NE)	SAMUEL G. DIMMOCK 1856-1860 (SE-NE)
CALEB COOK 1856-1860 (NW-SW)	DANIEL HIBBARD 1856-1859 (NE-SW)	DANIEL HIBBARD 1856-1859 (NW-SE)	DANIEL HIBBARD 1856-1859 (NE-SE)
CALEB COOK 1856-1860 (SW-SW)	DANIEL HIBBARD 1856-1859 (SE-SW)	DANIEL HIBBARD 1856-1859 (SW-SE)	DANIEL HIBBARD 1856-1859 (SE-SE)

Section 32, Township 38 N, Range 18 W
Wood River Township

CYRUS TRUE 1856-1859 (NW-NW)	CYRUS TRUE 1856-1859 (NE-NW)	HORATIO WOODMAN 1855-1857 (NW-NE)	HORATIO WOODMAN 1855-1857 (NE-NE)
CYRUS TRUE 1856-1859 (SW-NW)	CYRUS TRUE 1856-1859 (SE-NW)	HORATIO WOODMAN 1855-1857 (SW-NE)	HORATIO WOODMAN 1855-1857 (SE-NE)
EDW. M. HUNTER 1856-1859 (NW-SW)	HORATIO WOODMAN 1855-1857 (NE-SW)	HORATIO WOODMAN 1855-1857 (NW-SE)	HORATIO WOODMAN 1855-1857 (NE-SE)
EDW. M. HUNTER 1856-1859 (SW-SW)	HORATIO WOODMAN 1855-1857 (SE-SW)	HORATIO WOODMAN 1855-1857 (SW-SE)	HORATIO WOODMAN 1855-1857 (SE-SE)

Section 33, Township 38 N, Range 18 W
Wood River Township

More Early Settlers

	Born-Died	Country	Emig.	Land Description
Erickson, Zakarias	1828-	Sweden		NW ¼ Sec. 36, Twp. 38, R. 19W
Hauger, Hans J.	1834-1938	Asker, N.	1885	E½ W½ Sec. 26, Twp. 38, R. 19W
Hansen, Anton	1822-1906	Trondheim, N.	1864	S½ S½ Sec. 25, Twp. 38, R. 19W
Jacobson, Peder	1852-1935	Aafjorden, N.	1880	SW½ SW½ Sec. 27, Twp. 38, R. 19W
Johnson, Peter Juel	1857-1931	Hadsel, N.	1863	W½ SW¼ Sec. 23, Twp. 38, R. 19W
Johnson, Ole Andreas		Aafjorden, N.		E½ SW½ Sec. 27, Twp. 38, R. 19W
Mathison, Ole	1817-			E½ NE¼ Sec. 34, Twp. 38, R. 19W
Nelson, Magnus	1817-1902	(Sweden)	1862	NW¼ Sec. 24, Twp. 38, R. 19W
Olson, Andreas J. (Ole)	-1897			E½ W½ Sec. 23, Twp. 38, R. 19W
Olson, Thorsten	1841-1912	Halingdal, N.		Was druggist.
Pederson, Bersvend	1832-1913	Stjodalen, N.	1865	SW¼ NW¼ Sec. 23, Twp. 38, R. 19W
Pederson, Ole Aune	1827-1915			NE¼ SE¼ Sec. 35, Twp. 38, R. 19W
Skog, Anders G.	1820-1898	(Sweden)	1868	NW¼ NW¼ Sec. 26, Twp. 38, R. 19W
Skog, Anders G.	1820-1898	(Sweden)	1868	NE¼ NE¼ Sec. 27, Twp. 38, R. 19W

BIBLIOGRAPHY

A History of Burnett County Sheriffs by A. M. Anderson, Journal of Burnett County, 1933.

*An Encounter With Vesteralen_*Culture, Nature and History. Hansen, Oxem, Remen, and Bugge.

An Experience of Norway by Patrick Davis. Published in U.S. by David & Charles, Inc., 1974.

Enchantment of the World_Norway. By Martin Hintz. Children's Press, 1982.

Hadsel, the Heart of the Archipelago. Hadsel Municipality.

Land of the Midnight Sun. Book, 1&2, Paul B. DuChaillu, 1882.

Letter written in the Burnett County Sentinel by Peter A. Anderson, 1/30/1896.

Norway by Sigurd Hoel.

Norge-I Nord by Kåre Kleivan.

Norwegian Tourist Literature:

    Nordland.

    Nordland, Holiday Guide, 1998.

    Norwegian Coastal Voyage_Hurtigruten, 1995-1996.

    Norway, Official Travel Guide. 1996.

Of Norwegian Ways by Bent Vanberg_Harper & Row, 1970.

Olaf, Lofoten Fisherman by Constance Wiel Schram, E. M. Hale, 1929.

The Arctic Highway, A Road and Its Setting by John Douglas, David & Charles Newton Abbot, 1972.

The Land and People of Norway by Charbonneau & Landers.

The Nordlander Settlement in the Primeval Forest by Hjalmar R. Holand.

The Sami of Norway, Ministry of Foreign Affairs by Norinform, Elina Helander.

Troms, Norway, the Nature of Man, Troms Reiser.

Welcome to Bardu Roots Festival by Kjelle Hovde, 1987.

Index

About the Author

Born in Dent, Minnesota in 1907, Eunice Kanne began her formal education in country schools, and at Grantsburg high school. She graduated from River Falls Teachers College, the University of Minnesota and Northwestern University, where she earned her master's degree. Her teaching career began in the country schools of Burnett county in 1926 and has carried her to public schools in Wisconsin, Minnesota and Illinois. During World War II she was an instructor in radio communications for the United States Army Air Force in Madison. She later spent one year as a primary instructor with the U.S. Army in Germany. Her career as a researcher and writer of history began after she retired in 1972. *From Far North Norway* is her fourth book. It is about life in the part of Norway from which many early Grantsburg people came. It combines her love of history with her love of travel, which has taken her to sixty countries on six continents, including five trips to North Norway. She lives in Grantsburg.